KEEPING BLACK BOYS OUT OF SPECIAL EDUCATION

by Jawanza Kunjufu

African American IMAGES

Chicago, Illinois

Front cover illustration by Harold Carr

First Edition, Fourth Printing

Printed in the United States of America

ISBN: 0-974900-02-8

CONTENTS

117389

DEDICATION

This book is dedicated to all the African American boys who are in kindergarten. If you want to see God at His best, look at boys in kindergarten. They sit in the front of the class, they are eager, they are serious, and they want to learn.

While writing this book, I was informed that an African American male kindergarten student was reported to the police by the principal. He was handcuffed, taken out of the school, and—to intimidate him— driven around in a police vehicle! Where is the outrage? Unfortunately, as most school superintendents are aware, almost 60 percent of their African American male students in kindergarten will not graduate.

When I look at African American boys in kindergarten, I see future engineers, computer programmers, accountants, teachers, doctors, lawyers, ministers, and entrepreneurs. I see husbands and fathers. What do you see in these children? Whatever parents and teachers see in their children is usually what they will get.

My prayer is that no African American male in kindergarten will ever visit a special education class unless there is a hearing, sight, or physical impairment. I pray that every African American boy will grow up to be an educated, responsible Black male who will be an asset to his family and community.

While writing this book, my father, Eddie Brown, made his transition. I thank you daddy for teaching me about manhood, being dependable, and giving me high expectations.

To God Be The Glory

INTRODUCTION

Is there a relationship between special education and prison? Is there a correlation between cocaine and Ritalin? Is illiteracy a precursor to incarceration?

If I had the opportunity to talk to the late Thurgood Marshall, the famous lawyer who helped spearhead Brown vs. Topeka and the end of segregation in public schools, I would ask him, Has special education become the new form of segregation?

Why are African American males placed in special education more than any other group? Why are White females placed in special education the least? Why are White males placed in special education more than White females? Have we designed a female classroom and tried to shove in large numbers of male students?

Why is there a lesser chance of a male being placed in special education in Europe than in America? Is there any correlation between the low percentage of White females in special education and the fact that 83 percent of elementary school teachers are White females? Could the reason for the high placement rate of African American males in special education be that African American male teachers count for only 1 percent of all teachers in public schools?

Some scholars and authors have postulated that the reasons for African American males being disproportionately placed in special education are poverty, environment, and family background. If we accept this premise, and I do not, then why aren't African American females, who live in the same conditions, placed in special education at the same magnitude as African American males?

How do we explain the disproportionate percentage of African American children, particularly males, who are labeled—highly subjectively—to have conditions such as ADD (Attention Deficit Disorder), ADHD (Attention Deficit Hyperactivity Disorder), EMR [Educable Mentally Retarded], and LD (Learning Disabled)? Are scholars suggesting that poverty affects those disorders but not hearing, vision, and physical impairment, which can be more objectively diagnosed?

If you have read any of my books, you will know that I am extremely interested in solutions. My late mentor, Dr. Barbara Sizemore, gave me the theoretical paradigm that I use in my writings and consulting work for school districts nationwide. Simply, the paradigm is: problem, cause, solution, implementation. In a typical hour workshop, most people will spend 55 minutes looking at the problem, four minutes at the cause, one minute at solutions, and will return to the next workshop (if there is one) to come up with implementation strategies.

In my research on the plight of African American males being disproportionately placed in special education, I discovered an enormous amount of literature describing the problem. And it is a tremendous problem in America. African American males make up only 8 percent of the public school student population but constitute almost 30 percent of the students placed in special education.

While I do provide an analysis of this problem, which has global and far-reaching implications, you will find that the heart of this book focuses on solutions and implementation strategies. From this Introduction to the Epilogue, Keeping Black Boys out of Special Education is filled with numerous new understandings, solutions, and implementation strategies to remedy this national tragedy.

I am concerned about the field of special education. It was never designed to be a dumping ground for African American students, particularly males. When I meet educators who tell me they are special education teachers, I ask them, Why is there a disproportionate percentage of African American children in special education? Why the disproportionate percentage of African American male students? In fact, why are there more male students of all races in special education?

The situation is parallel to the one I encountered when I wrote *Countering the Conspiracy to Destroy Black Boys*. I felt compelled to write Conspiracy after visiting schools and observing large numbers of Black boys in special education, remedial reading, and the principal's office awaiting suspension.

As an outsider, I raised the simple question, Is this normal? Is this acceptable, and are there any plans to reduce the imbalance? When a people, an institution, or a country can live with a disease so long that they have come to accept it as normal, you know they are in trouble.

The disproportion of Black male students in special education is not normal, and it is not acceptable. Anyone who calls himself or herself a professional in this field should be embarrassed. They should be looking not for rationales to justify continuance of the problem but strategies to eliminate it.

Throughout this book, I will argue that one of the major reasons for African American males being disproportionately placed in special education classes is because the regular classroom is not culturally sensitive to the needs of this unique population. Neither is the special education classroom, for that matter. As a result, the problem has grown over the years. Both regular and special education classrooms must become sensitive to the cultural and developmental needs of African American male learners.

I am aware that many educators do not accept my premise. They feel the problem lies not with a culturally insensitive regular or special education classroom but with the dysfunction of the Black male child. In my service to schools, I help teachers and administrators develop strategies to close the racial achievement gap. The biggest hurdle I must overcome is raising awareness that there is indeed a problem and helping teachers and administrators see the errors in their perception and ways of doing business. Before seeing the light, however, without fail, they first want me to fix the children. Teachers are not the problem, they maintain. There are no deficiencies or shortcomings in their expectations, pedagogy, and/or curriculum. Black boys are the problem and need to be placed in a special education classroom because of their poor academic performance, emotional and physical immaturity, and poor behavior.

This book is my response to that erroneous thinking. Throughout, we will address teachers' concerns with the latest research on how boys mature, develop, and learn. We will look at research that shows how gender and racial prejudice have led to the disproportionate placement of Black boys in special education. And we will provide solutions and implementation strategies for the classroom and placement process.

The problem is not with Black children. Failure to understand the cultural and developmental needs of Black children is the problem. Public schools are failing not only African American males and females but also males of all races and ethnic groups.

I am reminded of the hearing conducted in 2001 by the U.S. House of Representatives' Committee on Education and the Workforce on the over-identification of minority students in special education. In his testimony, Representative Chaka Fattah concluded with the following story of Billy Hawkins.

For the first 15 years of his life, Billy Hawkins was labeled by his teachers as Educable Mentally Retarded. Billy was back-up quarterback for his high school football team. One night he was called off the bench and rallied his team from far behind. In doing so, he ran complicated plays. He clearly demonstrated a gift for the game. The school principal, who was in the stands, recognized that the retarded boy could play and soon after had Billy enrolled in regular classes. He instructed his teachers to give him extra help. Billy went on to complete a Ph.D. and is now an associate dean at a major university.[1]

Early in his elementary school career, my friend Les Brown was labeled mentally retarded and told that he would never amount to anything. For a good while, Les believed this and earned all Fs, flunking twice. It was only in high school, where he bonded with a high school teacher who cared about him, that this "mentally retarded" student became an honor roll student and went on to become one of the best communicators the country has ever witnessed.

Some educators believe that the best way to teach African American males is similar to the military approach of "break him down then build him up." How unfortunate it is that so many African American boys are having their spirits destroyed because some teachers believe in that approach to education and classroom discipline. Black boys are not horses, and they don't need to be broken down. Why not just build them up? As we will discover in this book, the track record for the "break him down then build him up" approach in regular and special education has not served the African American male student well at all. The solutions I present are all designed to build up

Black boys, and when a school commits to their implementation, they work.

At an NABSE (National Association of Black School Educators) conference, an educator and mother of a son told me that her son's spirit had been broken, that the kindergarten boy who was eager and loved learning had lost his zeal for learning. His spirit had been broken. Do you know what it is like when students lose their spirit? In the Mainstreaming Strategies chapter, we will look at options for teachers who do not know how to handle male students. For example, some children like to blurt out the answers without raising their hands.

I do not condone this behavior, but if I were a classroom teacher faced with two scenarios—a class of silent student zombies or a class of students who were so excited about learning that they blurted out answers—give me the latter over the former.

I told my colleague that she should never allow a school to break her child's spirit. She should do whatever she could to fight for her son. We will discuss ways that parents can fight for their sons in the chapter on Parent Empowerment. Parents should never allow a school to destroy and break the spirits of their sons.

Interestingly, this educator was also a parent. She understood what it was like to go against the system, her system, to protect her son. She realized how difficult it was to negotiate with and fight the system. She began to motivate her son. She had him read books by Les Brown and Malcolm X. She sat in on classrooms and observed teachers. She gave teachers my books to read. She identified her son's interests. When we later talked, she proudly reported that her son was now an honor roll student and on his way to Morehouse University and then law school.

Many students who are placed in special education are labeled ADD or ADHD. By stating that ADD is a medical disorder, experts place the burden and source of the problem on the child. Yet unlike other medical diseases such as diabetes or pneumonia, this is a disorder that pops up in one setting, only to disappear in another. Isn't it ironic that a Black boy may do just fine with one teacher, but in the next grade another teacher labels him hyperactive or with ADD? Is the problem with the boy or with an inconsistency between his teachers? Is there an inconsistency in how Black boys are assessed? How do we explain ADD as a medical disorder in a first-period class and not in a third-period class? In the chapter on Master Teachers, we will look at the phenomenon that 20 percent of the teachers make almost 80 percent of the referrals to special education.

How is it that Black boys who have been labeled ADD have the amazing ability to listen, remember, and repeat every word off a rapper's CD? In his excellent book *The Myth of the ADD Child,* author Thomas Armstrong says:

> I taught a remarkable group of kids during my five years in special education classrooms. They included a boy who held the national swimming record for breast stroke in his age group, a girl who was a model for a national department store chain, a boy whose science fiction sagas had us all wondering what he would think of next, a girl who was being investigated by parapsychologists for psychic abilities. Several students had superior artistic skills, kids who were natural leaders, mechanical wizards, musicians, mathematicians, and more. What they all had in common was difficulty with the traditional model of workbooks, lectures, and standardized tests, a difficulty that sometimes showed itself in learning problems, sometimes in behavioral or attentional.[2]

Imagine this: You are taken into a room and made to sit on a hard, wooden chair with a desk in front of it. You are not allowed to eat, drink, speak, or go to the bathroom. You are expected to stay in this room for six hours.

There will be two breaks, 10 minutes and 30 minutes. If you cannot follow these rules, you are given psychiatric drugs to control your behavior. Where are you? In a prison? No, you are in an American public elementary school! Could you endure the above scenario day in and day out? Do Black boys go there for several years and then return to the mainstream classroom at grade level? Just what makes special education special? In the next chapter, History and Terms, we will explain the original reason for special education and its current state.

CHAPTER 1: HISTORY and TERMS

In 1975, Congress passed Public Law 94-142, The Education of All Handicapped Children Act. It guaranteed that each handicapped child age 3 to 21 would receive a "free and appropriate" education in the "least restrictive environment" possible. This law became known as the Mainstream Law. Children with handicaps were to be educated in regular classrooms unless the nature and severity of their disability was so great that it could be demonstrated that they could not make progress in regular classes.

In 1990, Public Law 94-142 was retitled and expanded. It is now called The Individuals with Disabilities Education Act (IDEA Public Law 101-476). IDEA was amended in 1997 and in 2004. The amendment in 1997 (Public Law 105-17) gave greater powers to parents and their role in the educational process. Also in 1997, there was concern about the disproportionate percentage of African Americans and minorities being placed in special education classes.

The 2004 legislation (HR 1350) was connected with the Leave No Child Behind Act. This amendment places greater responsibilities on school districts to disaggregate their scores and to review thoroughly if there are a disproportionate percentage of minority students in special education. It states that every effort should be utilized to reduce the referrals of minority students into special education. Those placed in special education should be allowed the least restrictive environment, and measurable progress must be secured.

Whether the government is going to successfully monitor school districts that are out of compliance regarding the disproportionate placement of minority and African American students in special education is debatable. Whether the government is going

1

to put some financial teeth into the amendment and reduce funding for school districts that are out of compliance is yet to be determined.

ADD and ADHD

African American students who are placed in special education are routinely labeled ADD (Attention Deficit Disorder) and ADHD (Attention Deficit Hyperactivity Disorder). Whenever we see these diagnoses, our suspicions should be raised immediately. From the Diagnostic and Statistical Manual of Mental Disorders (4th edition), inattention and hyperactivity are defined as follows:

Inattention

Six or more of the following symptoms of inattention have persisted for at least six months to a degree that is maladaptive and inconsistent with developmental level.

A. Often fails to give close attention to detail or makes careless mistakes in schoolwork, work, or other activities.
B. Often has difficulty sustaining attention in tasks or play activities.
C. Often does not seem to listen when spoken to directly.
D. Often does not follow through on instructions and fails to finish schoolwork or duties in the workplace.
E. Often has difficulty organizing tasks and activities.
F. Often avoids, dislikes, or is reluctant to engage in tasks that require sustained mental effort, such as schoolwork or homework.
G. Often loses things necessary for tasks or activities (e.g., toys, school assignments, pencils, books, or tools).
H. Is often easily distracted by extraneous stimuli.
I. Is often forgetful in daily activity.

History and Terms

Hyperactivity

Six or more of the following symptoms of hyperactivity/impulsivity have persisted for at least six months to a degree that it is maladaptive and inconsistent with developmental level.

A. Often fidgets with hands or feet or squirms in seat.
B. Often leaves seat in classroom or other situations in which remaining in seat is expected.
C. Often runs about or climbs excessively in situations in which it is inappropriate.
D. Often has difficulty playing or engaging in leisure activities quietly.
E. Is often on the go or often acts as if driven by a motor.
F. Often talks excessively.
G. Often blurts out answers before questions have been completed.
H. Often has difficulty awaiting turn.
I. Often interrupts or intrudes on others.

In the more objective categories of hearing, vision, and physical impediments, there is no disproportionate percentage of African American males placed in special education. In the highly subjective categories, however, there is a disproportionate percentage. Notice how often the word "often" is used above to describe inattention, hyperactivity, and impulsivity. Can we quantitatively define "often"? For that matter, what is scientific (or magical) about six months? Why not seven? Why not three? If your behavior were being assessed, how would you be rated? Do you, from time to time, suffer from inattention or hyperactivity as defined above?

In one study, parents, teachers, and physician groups were asked to identify hyperactive children in a sample of 5,000 elementary school children. Approximately 5 percent was considered hyperactive by at least one of the groups while only 1 percent was considered hyperactive by all three groups. In another study, using a well-known behavior rating scale, mothers and fathers agreed only about 32 percent of the time on whether a child of theirs was hyperactive. Parent versus teacher ratings were even worse. They agreed only about 13 percent of the time.[3]

Such studies make all special education referrals suspect.

ODD

Oppositional Defiant Disorder is another category popular with high-referring teachers. Students with four or more of the following behaviors are considered ODD:

A. Often loses temper.
B. Often argues with adults.
C. Often refuses to comply with adult requests.
D. Often blames others.
E. Often is annoyed.
F. Often is vindictive.
G. Often is angry.
H. Often deliberately annoys people.

Characteristics of the Gifted and Talented

Many African American males are erroneously placed in special education, when in reality they possess the following gifted and talented characteristics:

1. Keen power of observation.
2. Sense of the significant.
3. Willingness to examine the unusual.
4. Questioning attitude.
5. Intellectual curiosity.

6. Inquisitive mind.
7. Creativeness and inventiveness.
8. High energy levels.
9. Need for freedom of movement and action.
10. Versatility.
11. Diversity of interests and abilities.
12. Varied hobbies.

Just how scientific are the assessment tools that determine whether a child has ADD, ADHD, or ODD? The studies show that principals, psychologists, social workers, physicians, regular teachers, special education teachers, and parents do not always agree about their children. It makes me wonder about the assessment tools themselves, the way they are used, and the appropriateness of their use in the referral process. If the tools were well-designed, then it would not matter who was making the observations or taking the tests; the diagnosis of the child would always be the same. Clearly that is not the case with tools currently being used.

Tests are often used as a mechanism of control. A decision maker can use test results to persuade and manipulate others to his or her point of view. Seldom is the design, relevancy, or appropriateness of the test questioned. The best-known case focusing on special education placement was the 1972 case of Larry P. vs. Riles. At the time, IQ tests were being used to place students in EMR (Emotionally and Mentally Retarded) classes. The defense argued that racial imbalance in the EMR classes was not the result of test scores since parental consent for placement was required. The court decided that the parents would also be influenced by the test scores and was not sympathetic to the defense's argument that there was no better alternative. The outcome was that neither the IQ nor any other test could be the sole determinant of whether a child is placed in special education. The Board of Assessment and Testing issued a report, concluding that the usefulness of IQ testing in making special education decisions needed reevaluation.

There are many, many tests available. Rather than carefully studying the tests to determine their accuracy and cultural appropriateness, educators and psychologists tend to use the same tests over and over. "Any test will do" seems to be the prevailing belief. Their approach to the assessment of Black boys' behavior and academic performance is careless and unscientific.

Unfortunately for many African American parents and even for educators, the cultural bias of these tests is often hidden. Below is a small sample of the many tests that are available to schools:

The Stanford-Binet IQ Test
The Kaufman Assessment Battery Scale
The Columbia Mental Maturity Scale
The Slosson Intelligence Test Revised
Test of Nonverbal Intelligence
The Woodcock Test
The Wechsler Intelligence Scale for Children
The Cognitive Assessment System
The Matching Familiar Figures Test
The Wisconsin Card Sort Test
The Bender Visual Motor Gestalt Test
Differential Aptitude Test Battery
The House-Tree-Person Technique
The Iowa Test of Basic Skills
The Minnesota Multiphasic Personality Inventory
The Otis Lennon Mental Ability Test
The Peabody Picture Vocabulary Test
The Stanford Achievement Test
The Vineland Social Maturity Scale
The Wide Range Achievement Test
The System of Multicultural Pluralistic Assessment
The Black Intelligence Test of Cultural Homogeneity
The Learning Potential Assessment Device

History and Terms

As you can see from the above list, and this list is not complete, numerous tests are available. Who determines which test is to be used? Are there any considerations for the cultural appropriateness of the test?

In the chapter on racial discrimination, we will review some of these tests for their cultural bias. We will also look at the tests that are more culturally appropriate for African American students.

I am reminded of the horror story of the child who was given an IQ test and only scored 79. Several weeks later, the same child was given the test in the format of a game and scored 121. When the child was relaxed and was told it was just a game, he scored 121. Based on the 79 score, the child was destined for special education. Based on the 121 score, the child was gifted and talented with the potential of running a multinational corporation or developing a cure for cancer. Which tells the true story of the child's cognitive ability?

Let us now review some popular terms that are often used in the special education field.

FAPE – Free Appropriate Public Education.

IEP – Individualized Education Plan. The IEP is a written plan for a child with a disability. We will discuss this in detail in a later chapter.

Inclusive – Includes students who receive the majority of their instruction in a regular classroom and receive special education and related services outside the classroom for less than 21 percent of the school day.

Least Restrictive Environment – The objective is for students to be in the mainstream regular classroom as much as possible.

Resource Room – Includes students who receive special education and related services outside the general classroom for at least 21 percent, but not more than 60 percent, of the school day.

Substantially Separate – Includes students who receive special education and related services outside the general classroom for greater than 60 percent of the school day. Separate classes, separate schools, and residential facilities are included in this classification.

In the chapters that follow, we will document that a disproportionate number of African American students, especially males, are placed in restrictive environments. We will review and analyze the IEP to determine whether or not it really is individualized.

In the special education field, the word "appropriate" is thrown around a lot. This word is as vague as "often." Is it appropriate to give a right-brain learner left-brain pedagogy? Is it appropriate to teach African American children false history, such as Columbus discovered America; Lincoln freed the slaves; Egypt is in the Middle East; and African American history began on a plantation in 1620?

There is a popular phrase in the industry: "Special education is a service, not a place." If we simply move students from one culturally insensitive regular classroom to another culturally insensitive special education classroom and expect a different outcome, that borders on insanity.

The following are some ideas that should be discussed in the industry:

ADDD – Attention to Ditto Deficit Disorder.
MTB – Material That's Boring
"Different" is not synonymous with "deficient."

ADD has been around ever since teachers attempted to teach students subjects that did not interest them. In most cases, it should not be described as a learning disability but as a teaching disability. Ronald Davis says in *The Gift of Dyslexia,* "Both our society and the world in general are becoming more visual. But many of our institutions, particularly our schools, have not kept up." Thomas Armstrong provides the following:

History and Terms

Some children are not suffering from ADD, but they suffer from rule governed behavior. These children are considered to be less responsive to rules established by authorities and less sensitive to the positive or negative consequences that authorities set down for them in advance. They're less likely, for example, to respond positively to statements like, "If you get out of your seat, then I will keep you in during recess," or "If you stay in your seat, I will give you a prize at the end of the day." In other words, kids labeled ADD will not play the game set down by the rule-making parents and teachers.

While a certain amount of rule following is necessary to maintain the social order, it is not always advantageous to be a rule follower. Witness the example of super obedience in Nazi Germany or the Jones massacre in California. The Euro psychologist Stanley Milgram's experiments in obedience suggest that human beings have a frightening capacity to follow orders when given by a respected authority.

Milgram had volunteers administer electric shocks to a subject in a control room every time the subject made an error on a learning task. With each subsequent error, the voltage level was increased. Despite protests from the subject, the volunteers were ordered to proceed to higher levels of voltage.

Statements like, "It is absolutely essential that you continue" and "You have no other choice. You must go on," were used by the experimenter in charge to pressure the volunteers into continuing to shock the subject. In actuality no real shock was given. The subject only pretended to be in pain. But the volunteers didn't know that, and fully 65 percent of them showed total obedience in administering the full range of shocks.[4]

We may want to contrast Oppositional Defiant Disorder with Overly Compliant Children.

In closing, Thomas Armstrong in *The Myth of the ADD Child* provides us with an excellent list of industry terms to compare and contrast.[5] Based on the bias of the teacher, the cup (the boy's behavior) could be half empty or half full.

Negative	Positive
Hyperactive	Energetic
Impulsive	Spontaneous
Distractible	Creative
A daydreamer	Imaginative
Inattentive	Global thinker with a wide focus
Unpredictable	Flexible
Argumentative	Independent
Stubborn	Committed
Irritable	Sensitive
Aggressive	Assertive
Attention Deficit Disorder	Unique

In the next chapter, we will look at the trends that are affecting the special education industry.

CHAPTER 2: TRENDS

Special education is now a
$60 billion industry.

*

Most schools have a
declining general population
but an increasing
special education population.

*

Twelve percent of all
public school students in America
are labeled special education students.

There are six million children
enrolled in special education.
There are four million males
and two million females.

*

Of African American students
recommended for special education,
92 percent are tested
and 73 percent are placed.

*

ADD and ADHD represent 50 percent
of the diagnoses of all children
placed in special education.

Trends

Thirty percent of special education teachers are unqualified, and the majority of them teach in African American schools.

*

Eighty percent of all students
referred to special education
are below grade level in reading.

*

Eighty-five percent of all special education students receive drugs.

Forty percent of special education students
receive education modifications,
but many say it is inadequate.

*

Only 27 percent of African American
male special education students
graduate from high school.

*

Only 41 percent of African American
male regular students
graduate from high school.

Trends

Forty percent of special education students become addicted to drugs.

*

Less than 10 percent of special education students return to and stay in mainstream classrooms.

*

Eighty percent of special education referrals are generated by teachers.

Twenty percent of America's teachers make 80 percent of the referrals into special education.

*

Eighty percent of special education students are deficient in reading and writing.

*

There is a four-to-one ratio of African American males to African American females in special education.

Trends

There is an average 40 percent achievement gap between special education and general education students (and this is with inflated scores due to testing accommodations for special education students).

*

Ritalin is the fifth leading drug in America after nicotine, alcohol, cocaine, and marijuana.

*

It costs $7,000 on average to educate a child in a regular classroom and $12,000 in special education.

The federal government promises to pay
40 percent of the special education
bill but historically has paid
less than 20 percent.

*

African American students comprise
17 percent of public school students
but constitute only 3 percent
of gifted and talented students,
African American males,
less than 1 percent.

*

Prisons project new construction
on current fourth-grade reading levels.

I'd like you to meditate on the above trends and seriously
ponder the implications as we move into the next chapter on racial
discrimination.

CHAPTER 3: RACIAL DISCRIMINATION

This could be a difficult chapter because in America we are not comfortable talking about racism. It is much easier to talk about classism or sexism than to talk about racism. This is unfortunate because you cannot solve a problem if you are in a state of denial.

I am often reminded of the liberal teacher in Seattle who told me after my workshop that she did not see color. She saw children as children. So I asked her if I could visit her classroom because I knew that bulletin boards, library collections, and décor do not lie. Her students were a mosaic of the country: 60 percent African American, 20 percent Asian and Hispanic, and 20 percent White. Yet she had an all-White Dick and Jane bulletin board, library collection, and lesson plans. The only color she saw was White.

This chapter will be difficult for educators, like the teacher in Seattle, if they are in a state of denial.

There are four stages we go through before solving any problem: We first deny, then admit, understand, and appreciate. Once beyond the denial phase, we must admit that race is a factor. We must honestly ask ourselves if there has been any discrimination against African American children in special education. Once we are able to admit to the racism and discrimination that exist in special education, we can begin to understand how racism is expressed in this industry. Finally, we must appreciate the racial and cultural differences of African American children, particularly males, so that we can reduce their disproportionate placement in special education.

My question to you, the reader, is Which stage are you in? Are you in denial of the problem? Have you admitted that there is a problem? Do you understand the nature of the problem? Do you appreciate the cultural uniqueness of your students?

I titled one of my earlier books *Black Students—Middle-Class Teachers*. Notice I did not say Black Students, White Teachers.

KEEPING BLACK BOYS OUT OF SPECIAL EDUCATION

I said Black Students, Middle-Class Teachers because there are "Negro" educators who, while they look Black, do not understand nor appreciate race and culture. I try my best in my integrated workshops to convey to White teachers that it is not the race or gender of the teacher but their expectations that is important to educating children.

A National Assessment of Title I documented that high-poverty schools have a greater percentage of inexperienced and uncertified teachers: 15 percent of elementary and 21 percent of secondary teachers in high-poverty schools had less than three years experience, compared with only 8 percent of elementary and 9 percent of secondary school teachers in low-poverty schools. In high-poverty schools, temporary or emergency certification accounted for 12 percent and out-of-field teachers for 18 percent of teachers, compared with low-poverty schools in which less than 1 percent of secondary school teachers had temporary or emergency certification or were teaching out of field.

Let us thoroughly explore racial discrimination in the field of special education. As African American children account for 17 percent of the school population, they should constitute 17 percent of the special education students and gifted and talented students. Ideally, 17 percent of the teaching force should be African American. More to the point, if African American males are 8.5 percent of the student body, they should represent 8.5 percent of special education students, gifted and talented students, and teachers. In each school, there should be a closer correlation between the number of Black students and Black teachers. If the school does not meet those figures, then the school should be deemed noncompliant and ineligible for federal funds.

What are the demographics in your school? What percentage of your students is African American? What percentage is African American male? What percentage of your special education and regular teaching staff is African American? What percentage of your gifted and talented students is African American?

The following three graphs tell the story because a picture is often worth a thousand words.

Racial Discrimination

Table 1. Compared to White Females
Identification Odds Ratios for Gender/Ethnicity Group

Gender	Ethnicity	MR Odds Ratio	LD Odds Ratio	SED Odds Ratio
M	American Indian	1.66	2.90	5.02
M	Asian American	0.50	0.78	0.91
M	Black	3.26	2.34	5.52
M	Hispanic	0.95	2.10	2.35
M	White	1.36	2.27	3.81

MR is mental retardation. LD is learning disability. SED is serious emotional disturbance.[6]

What is the reason why African American males have a 3.26 greater chance of being labeled mentally retarded than White females, a 2.34 greater chance of being placed in an LD classroom, and an astronomical 5.52 greater chance of being placed in an emotionally disturbed classroom? How do we explain this? Is this acceptable? How can it be prevented? How did it reach this magnitude?

The following is another chart that further reinforces the fact that discrimination exists in this industry.

Table 2. Comparison of Risk Ratios between Blacks and Whites in Hard and Soft Disabilities

States	Soft Disabilities			Hard Disabilities
	MR	ED	SLD	
Connecticut	4.76	2.62	1.49	1.49
Mississippi	4.31	0.94	1.72	1.07
South Carolina	4.30	2.04	1.26	1.30
North Carolina	4.08	2.76	1.10	1.03
Nebraska	4.08	6.06	1.69	1.50
Florida	3.91	2.14	1.20	1.09
Alabama	3.89	1.27	0.97	1.11
Delaware	3.61	2.45	2.55	1.30
New Jersey	3.60	2.40	1.28	2.18
Colorado	3.48	2.05	1.69	1.34
United States	2.88	1.92	1.32	1.18

Hard Disabilities include hearing, visual, and orthopedic impairments and traumatic brain injuries.[7]

It is interesting that in every state African American placement due to hard disabilities is less than placement due to soft
disabilities. Why is that? In Nebraska, African Americans have a 6
times greater chance than Whites of being placed in an ED class
but only a 1.5 times greater chance if placement is due to hard
disabilities.

For anyone who thinks this special education phenomenon
is reserved primarily for the traditional regions of racist activity,
i.e., the South, take a look at Nebraska, Connecticut, and Colo-
rado to see how this disproportionate percentage of African Americans placed in special education transcends any one region. To all
those who believe that African American poverty and family demographics drive special education placements, why aren't those
factors also present in placements due to physical disabilities? Why
are poverty and family demographics only linked to ADD, ADHD,
etc.?

The three terms "inclusive," "resource room," and "substantially separate" are also present in hotbeds of racist activity. Whites
have the greatest probability of being placed in an inclusive classroom and the least potential of being in a substantially separate
environment. In stark contrast, African Americans have the least
possibility of being placed in an inclusive classroom and the greatest potential of being placed in a separate environment. The following chart shows the racism that exists in these three categories.

National Racial Disparities in Inclusion

	Black (%)	Hispanic (%)	White (%)
Inclusive	37	42	55
Resource Room	30	30	29
Substantially Separate	33	28	16

8

Racial Discrimination

Earlier we presented the term "least restrictive environment." How do you explain that African American students are placed in the most restrictive "substantially separate" environments? The following research is an attempt to explain the disproportion of African Americans, especially boys, in special education. This is not Jawanza's opinion. This is research from acknowledged scholars.

Lanier investigated the links between teacher attitude, bias, race, and referrals to an educable mentally retarded (EMR) program. He gave 85 Black teachers and 274 White teachers four basic bogus profiles of possible EMR students. Some profiles were of Black students and some were of White students. Lanier found that the race of the student was significant when referring children to EMR classes. White teachers in the study referred Black students more often than White students whereas Black teachers referred Black students as often as they referred White students. This indicates that the race of a student plays a significant role in referrals to special education classes. What is more important is not the race of the victim but the race of the educator making the referral and the level of that educator's racial prejudice.

Tobias studied 199 teachers in New York City who were Black, White, and Hispanic. He discovered that teachers from the Hispanic group tried to keep children in the regular classrooms whereas White teachers recommended special education. Black teachers were less likely to refer a child if they knew the child was Black than if the child was White or Hispanic. Tobias noticed that teachers tended to refer students for special education services who were not of their own ethnic group more frequently than they did children of their own group or race.

Zucker and Prieto analyzed the affects of race and gender on teacher judgment concerning special class referral and placement. Their summaries suggest that teachers viewed special class placement as more suitable for Mexican American children than for White children.

Pernell studied student gender, teacher comments, socio-economic status, parent level of education, student academic performance, and social behavior variables as well as student-teacher ethnicity. He found that teachers were inclined to recommend African American males for special education placement more than any other student group.

Kaufman, Swan, and Wood concluded that teachers were less likely to agree with parents of Black male children in their perceptions of emotionally disturbed behaviors than the same teachers were in evaluating behaviors of White children.[9]

Jeanette Herrera, in *The Disproportionate Placement of African Americans in Special Education: An Analysis of Ten Cities,* reports that there is a relationship between the number of White teachers and the number of Black male students placed in special education. The cities with the highest percentage of White teachers had the highest percentage of Black students identified as special. For example, in New York City, 36 percent of students are Black, but 67 percent of the special education students are Black males. At the same time, White teachers are counted at 77 percent of the teachers in New York City. The following list ranks the cities from highest percentage of White teachers to lowest:

1. New York
2. Milwaukee
3. Miami
4. San Diego
5. Cleveland
6. Houston
7. Atlanta
8. Detroit
9. Chicago
10. Washington, DC

If we acknowledge that race is a factor and that racism is affecting the placement of African Americans in special education, then we either need to change the personnel making the referrals

Racial Discrimination

or change the behavior and thought processes of our existing teaching force.

Since the Brown vs. Topeka Board of Education case in 1954, there has been a 66 percent decline in African American teachers. Presently, only 7 percent of the American teaching core is African American while the student body is 17 percent. African American males account for only 1 percent of that teaching force, and the majority of them are employed in junior and senior high schools. Unfortunately, an African American boy can go to school from kindergarten to sixth grade without ever experiencing an African American male teacher.

The research clearly shows that there is an increasing percentage of African American students in special education, a decreasing percentage of African American teachers, and an increase in the percentage of White female teachers. The ideal solution would be to increase the percentage of African American teachers. But as I work with administrators nationwide, they often tell me that they cannot find African American teachers. While I acknowledge that there is an acute problem, I often ask them where they are looking.

Often administrators overlook the resources of more than 100 historically Black colleges. Although they only enroll 16 percent of African American college students, they produce 30 percent of African American graduates. Other places to look include the 85,000 Black churches, the Black fraternity and sorority annual conferences, the NAACP, and the Urban League. School administrators could also place ads on Black radio and in Black newspapers. If larger school districts are serious about remedying the shortage of Black teachers, they should hire Black advertising agencies to create marketing and advertising campaigns that would entice African Americans to pursue careers in education.

Several states have provided scholarships to African American male high school graduates to pursue education with the understanding that when they graduate they will return to that state and teach. I commend programs like the one in Clemson, South

Carolina: their Call Me Mr. program identifies and guides African American male college graduates who wish to pursue careers in education.

Make sure, though, that the African American teachers hired understand and appreciate Black culture. This is critical to success in a predominantly Black classroom.

The short-term reality, however, is that we must work with our existing staff. As Herrera's research discovered, in some cities, such as New York, literally three-quarters of the teaching body could be White. What can we do to help White educators make a thorough and culturally relevant assessment before placing children in special education?

For obvious reasons, lawyers try their best to have their clients tried by a jury of their peers. Witness the Rodney King and O.J. Simpson court cases in California and how perceptions of race can significantly cloud a situation.

If the police officers who beat Rodney King had been tried in Los Angeles, there may have been a different verdict. An African American/Hispanic jury in Los Angeles might have seen the beating differently from the White Simi Valley jury. If O.J. Simpson had been tried in White Simi Valley, the outcome of his case also would probably have been different. Wouldn't it be nice if the IEP team (we will discuss this in detail later) represented the racial make up of the student body?

How can we help the many White regular education teachers, special education teachers, social workers, psychologists, physicians, and administrators make fair decisions that are not racially biased and motivated? Will this require enforcement of IDEA? Will schools have to be threatened with the loss of federal funds before they do the right thing by Black boys?

The terms "different" and "deficient" are not synonymous. Insecure people believe that if someone is different from them, they are deficient in some way.

On the other hand, secure people are comfortable with differences. Educators like using terms such as "multicultural," "diversity," and "inclusion," but if we really understood the significance

Racial Discrimination

of these terms, there would be no disproportionate placement of Black boys in special education.

Special education was never designed to be a dumping ground for male students, in particular, African American male students. If we are sincere about multiculturalism, inclusion, and diversity, we need to honestly ask ourselves how we can use terms like "standard English," "classical literature," "classical music," "Third World," and "the Dark Continent" in good conscience.

Which English is standard? That spoken by Prince Charles in England, Ted Kennedy in Boston, or Jimmy Carter in Georgia? What is classical literature? I have visited predominantly Black schools where the classical literature of African Americans—Langston Hughes, Zora Neale Hurston, Toni Morrison, Gwendolyn Brooks—is still absent from the libraries and reading lists.

How about the term "Third World"—and what makes America First World? Do you rank societies based on gross national product, or do you rank them based on divorce, suicide, homicide, drug usage, or incarceration rates? Why are there are more than 265 negative definitions for "black" while virtually all positive attributes are assigned to "white"? What makes the continent that gave birth to mankind the "dark" continent? Why the implication that "dark" is bad, inferior, less than?

When I walk the halls of predominantly Black schools and hear educators use these terms and see the 46 pictures of White male presidents and no African or African American historical figures, I am concerned. This is a statement on what the staff thinks about their African American student body.

The Ideal Student

Why is there such a disproportion of African American males in special education? Could the reason be that the ideal student, the norm, the benchmark, the barometer that we compare all other students to is the White female student?

27

Remember, even White males are placed in special education at a far greater rate than White females.

As I study the statistics and research, I can only conclude that in the minds of many teachers, the White female is the ideal student. The following behaviors and attributes paint the profile of the ideal student.

- Quiet
- Can sit still for long periods of time
- A long attention span
- Can work independently
- Likes ditto sheets
- A left-brain learner
- Passive
- Cooperative
- Teacher pleaser
- Learned reading before the second grade
- Well developed fine motor skills
- Neat
- Good handwriting
- Well organized
- Likes multiple-choice exams
- Prefers departmentalization
- Speaks standard English
- Two-parent home
- Middleclass
- Mother works at home
- White
- Female

When you compare this list with the attributes of many male students (we will discuss this in detail in the Gender Learning Differences chapter) and consider the learning styles and culture of African American children, it is easier to understand why African

Racial Discrimination

American children represent only 17 percent of the school population but constitute more than 30 percent of the children in special education. It also becomes apparent why African American males represent almost 80 percent of African American children placed. If the White female is the ideal student, then many African American males—those who cannot be quiet or sit still for long periods of time, have a short attention span, cannot work independently or neatly on ditto sheets, are not organized, do not speak standard English, and prefer right-brain lesson plans—are in serious trouble.

Education is not a place but a service. If the objective of placing children in special education is to improve their academic and social skills, then we must ask ourselves whether we are trying to convert them into the ideal student or maximize their learning styles by making the necessary adjustments in special education classes. I do not accept the premise of many regular and special education teachers that the problem is with Black boys, so we must fix them, not the failing system. No matter how much you try, Black boys who have a healthy sense of their burgeoning masculinity will not develop into White girls. The more you try, the greater the devastation. The attempt to force such psychological programming on Black boys has had a catastrophic impact on their self-worth, family dynamics, community stability, and the socioeconomic system at large.

Assessment Testing

One of the major reasons why African American students are disproportionately placed in special education is because of America's over-reliance on IQ tests, many of which are culturally biased. Regard the following test questions, and you will see what I mean.

1. What was Washington's first name? Many African Americans would answer Harold or Booker T. On a culturally biased test, the only correct answer is George.

2. What color is a banana? Many African Americans would an-
    swer brown because, unfortunately, in many low-income
    communities bananas are no longer yellow. A child from an
    affluent community would probably answer yellow.

    Psychologist Robert Williams, the creator of the Black Intel-
ligence Test of Cultural Homogeneity, developed more than 100
assessment questions from an Africentric perspective. Here are
just a few of the multiple-choice questions.

1. H.N.I.C.
    A. Never intended color
    B. Head nigger in charge
    C. Have nothing in common
    D. Nodded in consent

2. Malcolm X's last name was:
    A. Little
    B. Jones
    C. Fanon
    D. Brown

3. Mother's Day
    A. Black Independence Day
    B. A day when mothers are honored
    C. A day the welfare checks come
    D. Every first Sunday in church

4. Oreo
    A. An intellectual
    B. An Uncle Tom
    C. A cookie
    D. A White liberal

Racial Discrimination

5. Vaseline is used for all but one of the following:
   A. Greasy, ashy legs
   B. Dressing hair
   C. First aid for minor bruises
   D. Relief for chest colds

Imagine if the Black Intelligence Test of Cultural Homogeneity was given to all students, including White students, and this was the sole determinant of whether a child would be placed in special education. An important outcome of the Larry P. vs. Riles decision is that IQ tests are no longer such a sole determinant. Unfortunately, these tests are still heavily relied upon, and many school districts choose tests that are culturally biased, naively thinking that all tests are equal. The following is a review of some of the more biased tests currently in use.

The Weschler Intelligence Scale for Children and the Cognitive Assessment System (CAS) were compared, using a sample of 78 White and African American students. All students were placed in special education programs for persons with mental retardation. Results showed that the Weschler scores were significantly lower than the CAS scores. Consequently, Weschler identified more children as having mental retardation than the CAS, 83 percent versus 57 percent, respectively. More importantly, Weschler classified disproportionately more African Americans (89 percent) than Whites (76 percent) as having mental retardation. The results imply that the problem of over-classification of African American children into special education classes due to mental retardation may be mitigated if the CAS were used instead of the Weschler.

The second most important finding was that the Weschler classified a much larger group of individuals as having mental retardation than the CAS. In other words, if the CAS replaced the Weschler as the common instrument of classification for mental retardation services eligibility, the number of African American and

White beneficiaries would drop by about 30 percent. Thus, the use of the CAS is a more conservative approach to placement.

The differential classification effect of the two tests across racial groups may be the result of their different content. The Weschler contains subtests that can be viewed as highly achievement loaded. The CAS does not include measurements of general information, vocabulary, and arithmetic. In addition, the CAS measures planning and attention, two scales that are not represented by the Weschler. These are important differences between the tests, which may have led to the differences in classification rates.[10]

Another test that I would highly recommend for those who are serious and sincere about reducing the number of African American males in special education is the System of Multicultural Pluralistic Assessment (SOMPA). This test is designed to assess the educational needs of children in a fair manner. The authors of this test are Jane Mercer and June Lewis.

SOMPA was designed to respond to the mandate of PL94-142, which is to assess the educational needs of children in a racially and culturally non-discriminatory manner. Construction and recommended usage of SOMPA are derived from a particular ideological view as to what society should be like, namely, culturally pluralistic. Thus, unlike most psychometric devices, the SOMPA authors openly express their ideological assumptions, e.g., intelligence and/or learning potential are distributed equally among all ethnic and racial groups; cultural pluralism will be promoted through use of the test.

The last test I would like to recommend is the Learning Potential Assessment Device (LPAD) created by Reuven Feuerstein. This is a dynamic cognitive assessment designed to evaluate the modest ability of students. The LPAD assesses a student's capacity to change his or her cognitive structures by means of learning. The LPAD does not measure individual performance by comparing it to accepted norms but, rather, assesses the person's learning

Racial Discrimination

potential. The results of LPAD assessments provide information about the student's learning capacity and possible achievement in the future and can lead to recommendations on how to realize that. The LPAD battery includes 15 series of tests aimed at assessing students' ability to modify their perception, memory, attention, logical reasoning, and problem solving.

Disenchantment with traditional testing practices and growing interest in the possibility that higher levels of cognitive functioning or intelligence can be taught has caused many psychologists to reconsider fundamentally the role of assessment in decision making and program planning for the low-functioning child. If intelligence is not an immutable quality but rather a capacity that can be targeted for development, consideration must be given to supplant the passive accepted approach to intelligence testing with an active modification and dynamic approach that can produce the prescripted information required to forge its enhancement.

In short, African American males should only be tested with the Black Intelligence Test of Cultural Homogeneity, the Cognitive Assessment System, and/or the Learning Potential Assessment Device. These tests will provide a more accurate assessment of the cognitive abilities of the Black male child. Iowa has chosen not to use IQ test because of their cultural bias. We encourage all other states to do likewise.

Inequities in Discipline

In *The Color of Discipline,* Professor Russell Skiba of Indiana University says that the determination factors for placing a child in special education, suspension, and expulsion are highly subjective. While White middle-income females receive warnings, low-income African Americans, especially males, receive special education, suspension, and expulsion. The following chart illustrates this disparity.

Subjective and Objective Criteria for Special Education, Suspension, and Expulsion

African American Males (subjective)
The teacher reports:

"He looked at me and made me feel uncomfortable."
"He rolled his eyes."
"I didn't like his attire [baggy pants]."
"He muttered under his breath."
"His walk."
"He shrugged his shoulders."
"He didn't respond fast enough."
"He didn't answer me."
"He raised his voice."
"He laughed when I disciplined him."
"He smiled when I disciplined him."

White Males (objective)
The teacher reports:

Fighting
Carrying a weapon (knife, gun)
Bloodshed

Clearly, Black male insubordination, along with being labeled inattentive or hyperactive, is highly SUBJECTIVE. This reminds me of an episode of the Oprah Winfrey Show. The White audience was divided into two groups: those with blue eyes and those who did not possess blue eyes. Those who did not possess blue eyes were treated royally before and during the show. Those who possessed the blue eyes were treated as second-class citizens. In less than an hour, the blue-eyed participants had become cynical, depressed, agitated, frustrated, and their self-esteem had been greatly reduced. This occurred during a mere hour. When we compare that to the treatment of African Americans from 1620 to the

Racial Discrimination

present, hopefully you will begin to understand the impact that racism can have on the psyche.

Children, like adults, believe in fairness. Black boys want to be treated fairly. Children in school should not be subjected to double standards. Public schools are breaking the spirit of African American males. How do you think a Black boy feels when he sees White children receiving warnings while he receives special education placement, suspension, or expulsion for behaving in similar ways?

A report from the Advancement Project titled "Derailed: The Schoolhouse to Jailhouse Track" confirms that states determine prison growth based on failing reading scores. How unfortunate it is that we believe it is better to incarcerate someone at $28,000 per year rather than teach a child to read for less than $1,000. Literacy is far cheaper than incarceration. The authors report that the schoolhouse to jailhouse track has damaged a generation of children, particularly children of color, in three significant ways:

1. Criminalizing trivial offences pushes children out of the school system and into the juvenile justice system. Even in cases where punishments are mild, students are less likely to graduate and more likely to end up back in the court system than their peers, and they are saddled with a juvenile or criminal record.
2. Turning schools into secure environments replete with drug sniffing dogs, metal detectors, and uniformed law enforcement personnel lowers morale and makes learning more difficult.
3. The negative effects of zero tolerance fall disproportionately on children of color and children with special needs.[11]

Consider these questions:

Have we created a schoolhouse to jailhouse track?
Is there a relationship between special education and prison?
Is there a correlation between Ritalin and cocaine?
Is illiteracy a precursor to incarceration?

We must do everything we can to derail these trends. One of the most effective weapons against Black male illiteracy and overall low academic performance is the master teacher. In the next chapter, we will briefly review the role of the master teacher in reducing the number of African American males in special education.

CHAPTER 4: THE MASTER TEACHER

The problem and the solution for the disproportionate placement of African American males in special education begin with the classroom teacher. Most referrals are not made by the principal, psychologist, social worker, or physician. Twenty percent of regular classroom teachers make 80 percent of the referrals. If we can correct the problem in the regular mainstream classroom, then possible 80 percent of our problem will be solved.

It is ironic that when Willie was in third grade with a master teacher, he was not labeled ADD or ADHD. But with an ineffective teacher in fourth grade, he is now being so labeled. We have come to accept this state of affairs, but there should be no difference in how a child is assessed from one teacher to the next. There may be relationship issues, but in terms of cognitive and behavioral assessments, there should be consistently applied standards from teacher to teacher. Subjective feelings should not enter into placement decisions.

If principals spent less time in the office and more time dealing with the 20 percent over-referring teaching population, we would eradicate this problem. Once a regular teacher has decided she wants a child removed from her class, it is very difficult for anyone on the IEP team to circumvent the process (we will discuss this in the IEP chapter). Again, the problem and the solution lie with the regular, mainstream classroom teacher.

My book *Black Students—Middle-Class Teachers* and the excellent research from the Education Trust both document how two consecutive years of an ineffective teacher can destroy a child for life. Let me repeat that: two consecutive years of an ineffective teacher can destroy a child for life. Children cannot be treated like yo-yos. Children do not have the resiliency to withstand a strong third grade teacher and an ineffective fourth grade teacher, with that cycle continuing throughout their educational careers.

I advocate looping master teachers, where the same teachers accompany students from grade to grade. I have known teachers who were so uncomfortable with the idea of their students going on to other teachers that they arranged to keep them from grade to grade—in some cases, from first or second grade to eighth grade graduation. I also encourage serial teaching. This requires several teachers per grade. A class of students will go from one master teacher to another.

How do we explain the success of looping and serial teaching? I promote this solution because it repudiates the myth that the problem is with the child and the home. If a child if blessed to have several years of study with a master teacher, all other risk factors become neutralized.

There are many types of teachers, as we will see below.

Types of Teachers

Unfortunately, not all teachers have equal skills. In *Black Students—Middle-Class Teachers,* I describe teachers in five categories: custodians, referral agents, instructors, teachers, and coaches. In her book *Other People's Children,* Lisa Delpit says a 12-year-old friend told her that there are three types of teachers:

1. Black teachers, who are not afraid of Black kids.
2. Most White teachers, who are afraid of Black kids.
3. The remaining few White teachers who are not afraid of Black kids.[12]

In *Dreamkeepers,* Gloria Ladson-Billings describes teachers in the following six categories: custodians, referral agents, tutors, general contractors, conductors, and coaches.

The Master Teacher

1. Custodians do not believe that much can be done to help their students and do not look to others to help them maintain classes.
2. Referral agents do not believe that much can be done to help their students improve, and they shift their responsibility to other school personnel by sending children to the school psychologist or the special education teachers.
3. Tutors believe that students can improve and that it is their responsibility to help them do so.
4. General contractors also believe that improvement is possible, and they look for ancillary personnel aids, resource teachers, and others to provide academic assistance rather than take on the responsibility themselves.
5. Conductors believe that students are capable of excellence, and they assume the responsibility for ensuring that their students achieve that excellence.
6. Coaches also believe that students are capable of excellence, but they are comfortable sharing the responsibility of helping them achieve with parents, community members, and students.[13]

Michael Porter, in the book *Kill Them Before They Grow,* describes teachers in five categories: people person, touchy feely, plantation mistress, theoretician, and missionary.

1. The people person truly believes that all children, especially African American children, can learn, and she tries very hard to help them learn. She respects African American parents and grandparents and is open to Africentricity.
2. Touchy feely White females constantly perform subtle anatomical examinations on the African boy. This female, because of stereotypes of African men, explores fantasies, even on a mental plane.
3. The plantation mistress has a hands off policy. She really can't stand even being near African American students. She is often conceited. She desires a transfer to a White school or a career change.
4. The theoretician is well versed in every Eurocentric theory and will use all of them on African American students.

5. The missionary persuades African American parents to assign their "culturally deprived" children to her because her way is better and she will save their soul.[14]

One of the major factors driving the disproportionate placement of African American males in special education is poor classroom management. The problem may not be with the behavior of African American males. It may be with teachers who have poor classroom management techniques. There are four types of challenging students:

1. Children who misbehave to get attention. They are trying to feel significant and create a sense of belonging by drawing attention to themselves. "I want you to notice me and care about me."
2. Children who misbehave to achieve power. Here, children are trying to feel important and connected to others by asserting themselves in a strong way.
3. Children who misbehave to seek revenge. Here children want to compensate for feelings hurt by deprivation of importance or sense of belonging.
4. Children who misbehave to assume an attitude of inadequacy. In this case, children are reacting to perceived loss of importance and belonging by simply giving up.[15]

The importance of the teacher's ability to manage the classroom is reinforced by findings in a longitudinal study of 1st grade students and teachers randomly assigned to classrooms in 19 schools. Boys who were aggressive in 1st grade were found to have a far higher probability of exhibiting behavior problems in later years if they were in poorly managed classrooms than boys who were similarly aggressive at the outset but were in well-managed classrooms.

The Master Teacher

Orfield provides the following analysis:

Classroom ecology is a critical issue that needs to be researched in much more detail. Kellam, Ling, Merisca, Brown, and Ialongo demonstrated that the experience of a disorderly classroom atmosphere in the first grade predicted a trajectory of increasingly aggressive behavior for boys who were initially resistant to school discipline. Our research has several examples of children referred for potential behavior disorders who are coming from classrooms where disorderly behavior is the norm because of the teacher's lack of skills.

Researchers have identified a variety of school-based risk factors that contribute to negative developmental outcomes. These minefields can contribute to existing risk factors and further increase the risk of poor social outcomes.

For example, poorly managed schools can be a risk-prone context for children with behavioral problems who frequently generate hostile and punitive reactions from teachers and peers and where early anti-social behaviors are reinforced by inappropriate school responses.

Schools can also be a place where students at risk for behavioral problems get caught up in a self-sustaining cycle of classroom disruption and negative consequences. This cycle includes academic failure as teachers ignore or are unable to address the academic needs of students with behavioral problems and force segregation with anti-social peers, which often reinforces problem behaviors. Finally, schools can frequently be settings for public humiliation as children and youth experience academic failure, peer rejection, and adult sarcasm. Black students are also more likely to attend schools characterized by practices that contribute to the development or escalation of anti-social behavior, such as:

- Ineffective instruction
- Inconsistent and punitive school-wide classroom and individual behavior-management practices
- Lack of opportunity to learn and practice pro-social, interpersonal, and self-management skills
- Unclear rules and expectations regarding appropriate behavior
- Failure to correct rule violations and reward adherence to them
- Failure to assist students from backgrounds that place them at risk for not bonding with the schooling process[16]

Caseau, Luckasson, and Kroth offer a number of other possibilities for the over-representation of African American males in special education. Male educators seem to have greater tolerance for rule violations, with male regular education teachers referring students with high levels of disruptive acting-out behavior less often than their female colleagues.

In support of these findings, Ritter also found female teachers to be more sensitive to externalizing behaviors in the general education classroom. Even when the behaviors of boys are identical to those of girls, teachers respond more emphatically when boys misbehave.[17]

The Master Teacher

The problem could be resolved with the development of more master teachers.

Listed below are some of the attributes of the master teacher.

- Knowledgeable about subject matter.
- Provides lesson plans congruent between pedagogy and learning styles and incorporates written, oral, visual, physical, and fine arts elements.

The Master Teacher

- Bonds, motivates, enhances self-esteem.
- Listens to students and is in proximity to all students.
- Décor of classroom is inspirational and culturally reinforcing.
- High level of self-respect keeps students from being distracted or sleeping.
- High expectations transcend race, income, gender, and appearance.
- Equitable response opportunities for all students.
- Equitable feedback for all students.
- Maximizes time on task.
- Assertive, consistent, complimentary, and clearly establishes rules and consequences.
- Provides cooperative learning experiences.
- Attempts to make curriculum relevant.
- Provides practical experiences, field trips, and role models.
- Students ask more questions than the teacher does.
- Develops critical thinking skills by asking open-ended questions.
- Enthusiastic about discussing course material.
- Writes legibly on the blackboard and on student papers.
- Speaks clearly, understandably, and calmly.
- Never intimidates or embarrasses students.
- Is readily available for consultations with students.
- Treats all students with respect and assigns room captains.
- Returns assignments in a reasonable time.
- Slows down when discussing complex and difficult topics.
- Is consistently well prepared and organized for class.
- Is aware of what material has been covered in previous classes.
- Is well prepared to answer questions.
- Dresses professionally.
- Subscribes to educational journals.

- Enrolls in classes to improve his/her craft.
- Reserves an area for tardy and unruly students.

The most significant characteristic of master teachers is not their race or gender but the expectations they have of their students.

- Students need teachers who will make them learn. A multicultural teacher must have multicultural values.
- Teach on your feet, not in your seat. If you listen and observe children , they will tell you how to teach them.
- It is a teacher's job to inspire students, especially if they lack motivation to learn. Telling is not teaching. I don't become what I think I can. I don't become what you think I can. I become what I think you think I can!
- Understand the difficulties your students have in the community and at home, but refuse to victimize them further by making excuses for them in the classroom. If a student has not learned, the educator has not taught.
- No significant learning occurs without a significant relationship.

The mediocre teacher tells. The good teacher explains. The superior teacher   demonstrates. The great teacher inspires.

- Effective teachers use a relevant curriculum that involves critical thinking and pedagogy that will produce tomorrow's leaders.
- You cannot teach what you do not care about to people you do not care about.
- In the ideal classroom, teachers and students listen to each other, and they work together on real problems. Teachers become facilitators and students discover answers.

The Master Teacher

Best practice research recommends the following:

- Less whole-class, teacher-directed instruction (lecture).
- Less student passivity: sitting, listening, receiving, and absorbing information.
- Less presentational one-way transmission of information from teacher to student.
- Less prizing and rewarding of silence in the classroom.
- Less classroom time devoted to fill-in-the-blank worksheets, dittos, workbooks, and other seat work.
- Less student time reading textbooks and other seat work.
- Less student time reading basal readers.
- Less attempt by teachers to thinly cover large amounts of material in every subject.
- Less rote memorization of facts and details.
- Less emphasis on competition and grades in school.
- Less tracking or leveling of students into ability groups.
- Less use of pull-out special programs.
- Less use of and reliance on standardized tests.
- More experiential, inductive, hands-on learning.
- More active learning in the classroom, with all the attendant noise and movement of students talking and collaborating.
- More diverse roles for teachers, including coaching, demonstrating, and modeling.
- More emphasis on higher-order thinking.
- More in-depth study of a smaller number of topics.
- More reading of real text.
- More responsibility transferred to students for their work, goal setting, record keeping, monitoring.
- More choice for students (e.g., choosing their own books, writing topics, team partners, and research projects).
- More enacting and modeling of the principles of democracy in school.

- More attention to effective needs and the varying cognitive styles of individual students.
- More cooperative, collaborative activities, to develop the classroom into an interdependent community.

Rules of Thumb

Rule 555. Master teachers abide by two important rules. The first is Rule 555. Experience has taught them that 95 percent of classroom problems are generated by 5 percent of students. Master teachers realize how important it is to identify that 5 percent. They find creative ways to bond with that 5 percent and direct their bad behavior into good leadership skills.

They make these students room captains, have them collect papers, and assign them other classroom duties. Master teachers understand that these children, especially boys, are seeking attention and/or power. They are going to be either your best students or your worst students, so master teachers do everything in their power to make them their best students.

Master teachers have learned that discipline problems occur primarily during the first five and last five minutes of the class period. I wonder how many African American boys have been suspended or recommended for special education because they were acting up in the first five minutes when the classroom teacher was trying to get organized. I am a stickler for time on task, and I am concerned about regular classroom teachers who are talking on their cell phones in school, answering e-mail in class, and talking to their colleagues across the hall instead of implementing the lesson plans when the class period begins.

Children are quick to recognize when a teacher is not prepared to teach. Master teachers are aware that they can circumvent 95 percent of their problems if they are prepared when students walk in the door. I suggest a daily math word problem, a daily Black history fact, and the assignment for the first period on the board.

Managing the last five minutes of classroom time is important. In a typical scenario, a teacher will give an assignment for the last 30 minutes of the period. Some students finish the assignment quickly, with minutes to spare. If the teacher has not provided additional work or structure for those students, they may exhibit behavioral problems because they have nothing to do. Master teachers are always prepared to assign additional work or allocate an area of the room where children can immerse themselves in other activities.

Remember, behavior problems may be traceable to poor classroom management rather than African American boys.

Rule 110. Before integration in 1954, Black teachers, progressive White teachers, and Black parents used to teach their children that in order to do well in America, they needed to score better than 80, 90, or even 100 on tests and assignments. Black children needed to be better than the best. Thus, Rule 110. Teachers had high expectations of their students, and they did not accept inferior work or allow social promotion. They did not consider poverty, home life, or race in the teaching of Black children. It never would have occurred to them to think like that.

We need to return to the era when being Black meant being the best. It has gotten so bad, as I wrote in *To Be Popular or Smart: The Black Peer Group,* that when Black children do well in school they are teased and accused of acting White. Boys are accused of being feminine. This is pure self-hatred. If being smart is acting White, then how do you act Black? If speaking proper English is speaking White, then how do you speak Black?

Before 1954, seldom did you hear Black youth associate being smart with being White. This is a phenomenon that took place with integration, and we need to rid ourselves of any low expectations that allow Black youth to think that way.

In the next chapter, we will discover that the solution to Black boys' behavioral and academic problems lies not in special education. We must teach them how to read.

CHAPTER 5: A READING OR A SPECIAL EDUCATION PROBLEM?

Eighty percent of students who are recommended for special education placement are below grade level in reading.

Sixty-three percent of African American fourth grade students are below grade level in reading.

Seventy-four million Americans read below the eighth grade level.

Eighty-five percent of juveniles coming before the courts are functionally illiterate.

Seventy percent of prison inmates are illiterate.

America as a whole has a serious illiteracy problem. It has been said that when White America has a cold, Black America has pneumonia. Illiteracy is more acute than pneumonia among African Americans and has reached epidemic levels for African American males.

Do we have a reading problem or a special education problem? Public Law 94-142 (1975) was designed to ensure that all children, primarily those who have hearing, visual, and physical impairments, would receive a quality education. Special education was not designed to be a dumping ground for children, primarily African American males, who have not mastered reading by third grade. If it were, we should dismantle special education and reclassify it as remedial reading. We should allocate as many resources as possible to address why so many Americans, particularly African Americans and African American males, have such difficulty with reading. Increasing the number of special education teachers may not be the correct approach to solving this problem. America needs to increase the number of reading specialists.

Has America always had a problem with literacy? The answer is no. There was a steady rise in literacy during early settling years and then a dramatic fall in the literacy rate. The Puritans and pilgrims had a high literacy rate because they wanted to know the Bible. Many learned to read by using the Bible as their only text.

(A personal note: Prayer was taken out of schools in 1962. The very next year, SAT scores declined for the very first time and teen pregnancy increased. How unfortunate that a country that was founded on biblical principles has now removed the Bible, prayer, and the Ten Commandments in schools. But that's another issue for another book.)

By 1930, the illiteracy rate had dropped to 4.3 percent, according to the U.S. Census. Can you imagine, in 1930 America had an illiteracy rate of about 4 percent. Yet today, our illiteracy rate has increased to almost 42 percent, with almost 74 million Americans illiterate. What has happened to the country?

If public schools want taxpayers to agree to additional funding, then schools must remedy this problem. If schools say the reason for illiteracy is poverty, social problems, learning disabilities, or the nine-month school year, how do we reconcile those same factors being present in 1930, when illiteracy was only 4 percent? While we could argue that television has not been helpful in raising literacy rates, we cannot totally blame television for the increase from 4 to 42 percent, or 74 million Americans.

Learning to Read

At what age are boys, particularly Black boys, expected to learn how to read?

At what grade level will they be placed in special education if they have not learned to read? I offer the following three scholars to further explain why it has become cruel to expect children, particularly boys, to master reading by the magical age of seven or eight, with the threat of special education if they do not.

A Reading or a Special Education Problem?

Dan Kindlon and Michael Thompson wrote in *Gender in Education* the following:

> Some researchers have suggested that the preponderance of boys among the learning disabled (60 to 80 percent) would disappear if eight-year-old boys were taught in classes with six-year-old girls because learning disabilities are diagnosed based on assessment of reading ability at a certain age. If you start teaching reading at an early age, it looks as if all your boys have reading disabilities. In short, the early age at which we teach reading favors girls on average and puts boys at a disadvantage. We probably shouldn't waste time because reports really all say the same thing. The kid who has trouble learning to read in first grade, starts to hate school, his self-esteem goes to hell, and when he's a teenager, he's pissed off or taking drugs. "We expect too much of boys and sometimes we don't expect enough," said a second grade teacher, reflecting on the way our culture's view of boys often scrambles messages they get from parents and teachers. On the one hand we expect them to do things they are not developmentally ready to do, and [on the other hand] to be tough little men when they're just little boys who need good-bye hugs and affection.[18]

In the excellent book *Right Brain Children in a Left Brain World,* Jeffery Freed provides the following:

> Anecdote after anecdote suggests that many brilliant people learned to read late in their grade school years. One might ask what difference does it really make when your child learns to read. The well-known educator Carlton Washburn did a famous study in the 1930s of children in the public schools

in Winnetka, Illinois. He compared classes of children who were introduced to formal reading instruction in the first grade with those who weren't introduced to reading until second grade. The children who started earlier had an initial advantage on reading tests used to chart people's progress, but the advantage totally disappeared by the time the children were in grade four. The most revealing part of the study came years later when the subjects were in junior high school. The evaluators didn't know which children had been in the first grade reading group and which ones in the second grade group. Observers were asked to look at all facets of the students' reading behavior. The study reached a very dramatic conclusion. The adolescents who were introduced to reading late were more enthusiastic, spontaneous readers than those who began reading early.

These data were also supported by the educational research of other countries. David Elkind writes in The Hurried Child that in Russia, formal education and instruction do not begin until children are age seven and yet Russian children seem far from intellectually handicapped. Early reading then is not essential to becoming an avid reader, nor is it indicative of who will become successful professionals. Elkind says that forcing children into early reading can actually have detrimental, long-term effects on children's academic performance and enthusiasm for learning. He asserts that children who are pushed to read before they have the requisite abilities to do so can develop long-term difficulties.

Elkind theorizes that it also seems as if reading has been foisted upon them at great cost in time and effort without their having any real understanding of the value of what they were learning. They showed the apathy and withdrawal that are frequent among children who are pushed too hard academically.

A Reading or a Special Education Problem?

> Before we became obsessed with fast—
> tracking kids and forcing everyone to read in first
> grade, children learned to read in their own good
> time at about eight years of age. In years past, we
> didn't make such a fuss about the child who failed
> to read until third grade. Perhaps in our more agrar-
> ian society a higher premium was placed on
> children's mechanical skills and abilities to do spe-
> cial tasks. We weren't as likely to label children
> who were late readers as "slow," "learning dis-
> abled," or "late bloomers."[19]

Lastly, on this subject of the magical age when we expect
children, particularly boys and African American boys, to master
reading, I offer the research of Michael Gurian in his excellent
book *Boys and Girls Learn Differently.*

> At this early education stage we have found that
> many or most learning disorders can be "cured"
> by rethinking expectations of the child's learning.
> For example, our educational culture is relatively
> obsessed with learning through early reading and
> labels nonreaders as disordered or behind. How
> much of this is cultural expectation? In Hungary,
> reading is not generally taught until the child is
> seven years old. Hungary consistently tests out at
> the high end of European countries in its children's
> reading skills by third, fifth, seventh, and later
> grades. Sweden's culture of literacy is similar. Ob-
> viously then, learning disorder diagnoses in the first
> six years of life can depend on the culture's expec-
> tations. Since males have a disadvantage in learn-
> ing to read early, it is no wonder that so many in
> the United States are diagnosed with a learning dis-
> order in the area of reading and writing. Rethinking
> expectations can rethink diagnoses.[20]

Educators and administrators should rethink the paradigm that dictates their special education referrals in light of the above research. If a child has a reading problem, then let's connect him with a certified reading specialist. Reason dictates against an immediate resort to a special education referral.

Children do not learn to read at the same rate, yet we declare that if a child has not learned to read by age eight or the third grade, he or she has a learning disability. Why have different learning rates become a special education issue? We need to rethink the position that children must learn to read at the same rate and point in time.

It is commonly accepted that boys and girls learn at different rates, but this knowledge has not changed our curriculums or referrals into special education. We will discuss gender learning differences in more detail in a later chapter, but for now I must raise the question: Why do we expect boys to perform at the same level as girls, in particular in the area of reading?

I recommend that a child should not be placed in special education for a reading disorder until grades four, five, and six. There is enough research to document that America has been premature in placing large numbers of children, particularly boys and Black boys, in special education.

The Phonics vs. Whole Language Debate

Why can't Johnny read? Teaching children to read and write can be complicated because English is neither a purely phonetic language (like Spanish) nor a purely symbolic language (like Chinese). It is a combination of the two. Approximately 13 percent of English words are unpredictable in their letter-sound relationship, such as the au in the words laugh and audible. In contrast, 50 percent of the words are very predictable. The remaining 37 percent consist of complex spelling that can be taught.

A Reading or a Special Education Problem?

Phonics can be helpful with the 50 percent of words whose pronunciations are predictable and the 37 percent of words with complex spelling patterns. The authors of *Best Practice* argue that phonics is not reading. Reading means gleaning understanding from print. Reading is not phonics, vocabulary, or other decoding skills, as useful as these activities may be. Reading is a transaction between the words of an author and the mind of a reader during which meaning is constructed.

The main goal of reading instruction must be comprehension. Above all, we want students to understand what is on the page. Reading is a process. Reading is a meaning-making process, an active, constructive, creator-higher order thinking activity that involves distinctive cognitive strategies. Before, during, and after reading, students need to learn how skillful, experienced readers actually manage these processes.

Beginning reading instruction should provide children with many opportunities to interact with print. These include listening to stories, participating in shared book experiences, making language-experience stories and books, composing stories in play, enacting dialogue, and reading and writing predictable books. These are just some of the many methods that are advocated in the whole-language philosophy, which looks at the larger picture and has a disdain for those who advocate phonics, who want to reduce reading simply to a technique for attacking words rather than developing a larger appreciation of language arts.

This debate has raged for almost a century, yet it fails to explain the decline in literacy from 1930 to the present and the fact that special education is being populated by male children who have not mastered reading by the age of seven. I offer the following research studies by respected groups that address this debate between phonics and whole language.

The National Reading Panel, a congressionally mandated independent panel under the auspices of the National Institute of

Child Health and Human Development, released its recommendations for reading instruction. The members of the panel based their findings on the largest, most comprehensive evidence-based review ever conducted of research into how children learn to read. The panel selected approximately 100,000 reading research studies published since 1966 and another 15,000 that had been published before that time. The panel relied solely on experimental and quasi-experimental studies and among those considered, only studies meeting rigorous scientific standards. Here are their conclusions.

Effective reading instruction includes teaching children to break apart and manipulate the sounds of words (phonemic awareness); teaching them that these sounds are represented by letters of the alphabet that can be blended together to form words (phonics); having them practice what they learned by reading aloud with guidance and feedback (guided oral reading); and applying strategies to guide and improve reading comprehension.

The panel's research suggests that reading instruction is complex. Children come into the classroom with different levels of preparation, as do their teachers. Not all children learn in the same way. One strategy does not work for all children. In addition, learning to read requires a combination of skills, including phonics, phonemic awareness, fluency, and comprehension skills.

The final results of the panel's findings demonstrate that learning phonics skills is critical for positive reading development. The panel determined that systematic phonics instruction leads to significant positive benefits for students in kindergarten through sixth grade and for children with difficulty learning to read. Kindergarteners who receive systematic beginning phonics instruction read better and spell better than other children. First graders are better able to decode and spell words. The students also show significant improvement in their ability to understand what they read. Similarly, phonics instruction helps older children spell and decode text better.

A Reading or a Special Education Problem?

Since the passing of the No Child Left Behind Act, educational research has been a hot topic. But research into reading over the last 20 years has been remarkably consistent. Independent researchers from all across the country have come to the same central conclusion: Early, explicit instruction in phonemic awareness and decoding is the key to reading success.

- Early means starting reading instruction in kindergarten or, even better, in preschool.
- Explicit means teaching specific skills, not leaving it up to kids to discover how to read or, all too often, not read on their own.
- Systematic implies a research-based plan for teaching kids how to read that builds on previously learned skills.
- Phonemic awareness is being able to distinguish the different sounds within a word.
- Decoding is sounding out a word and attaching meaning to the word.

Dr. Foorman described a study in which 262 children were randomly assigned to a kindergarten curriculum that focused on the explicit, systematic teaching of phonemic awareness and sound-spellings correspondence (Open Court reading series) to a standard curriculum that consisted of developmentally appropriate practices described by the state of Texas' Essential Elements for Kindergarten. Assessments indicated that this form of instruction was more effective in reducing reading disabilities than was instruction in a print-rich environment typified by interesting stories. The children in the explicit instruction curriculum made significant gains in phonemic awareness over the year. The greatest gains occurred when explicit instruction involved teaching sound-spelling correspondences along with phonemic awareness.[21]

The recent International Reading Association (IRA) position statement shocked many in the reading community, who, rightly or wrongly, had seen the IRA as the bastion of the whole language movement. The organization took a stance supporting phonics within a whole language program. As for the role of phonics in reading instruction, the IRA maintains that...

> The teaching of phonics is an important aspect of beginning reading instruction.Classroom teachers in the primary grades do value and do teach phonics as a part of their reading program. Phonics instruction, to be effective in promoting independence in reading, must be embedded in the context of a total reading/language arts program.[22]

In the book *Turning the Tide of Illiteracy,* the authors point out that both Cuba and Israel discovered that they had high illiteracy rates after using whole language methods. Both solved their problem by returning to intensive phonics. Fortunately for them, both are small countries, and once they found a solution, they implemented it nationwide and received immediate results.

There are some excellent reading programs on the market. If you are serious about addressing the reading problem in America, consider using materials from Open Court, Hooked On Phonics, Go Phonics, Modern Curriculum Press, or the Orton-Gillingham program in your classroom, home, or after-school reading program.

The Orton-Gillingham, which is based on sound, theoretical principles with a systematic, multisensory, phonetically based approach, is highly effective for teaching reading, spelling, and handwriting to learners of all ages. This diagnostic method analyzes a student's strengths and weaknesses and can help those who have not succeeded using other reading methods. It can be used to teach both beginning readers and those who have "holes" in their knowledge

A Reading or a Special Education Problem?

and skills. Structured and sequential teaching ensures that the individual student experiences continuous and visible success.

The Orton-Gillingham approach to language instruction addresses the simplest sound-symbol relationships and logically integrates the auditory, visual, and kinesthetic elements to reinforce optimal reading and spelling skills.

Students learn the basic building blocks of the English language, the phonemes, and then progress to syllables and word parts, such as prefixes, roots, and suffixes. In spelling, they learn the many spelling rules that govern the language. The Orton-Gillingham lesson plan integrates reading and spelling skills and builds through continuous practice and review. Students progress from the smallest elements of the language to reading books and applying their spelling skills when writing sentences. This method is particularly effective for students who have the following difficulties:

- Making sounds with the associated letters.
- Find it difficult to sequence sounds.
- Read aloud in an uneven, halting manner.
- Frequently skip over words.
- Fail to notice punctuation.
- Have difficulty remembering spelling patterns.

Hopefully the above-cited research will end this debate between phonics and whole language. Even the whole language advocates acknowledge that you cannot read without an understanding of the alphabet and its sounds. If phonics is not taught, is not taught for an adequate amount of time, or is taught poorly, it does not matter whether the child is 5 or 15, he or she will not be able to move on to whole language until phonics is mastered.

There is no need for this discussion to be "either-or." As Best Practice mentioned, whole language reading is not phonics. But in order to learn how to read, children must first be able to understand the alphabet and its sounds and develop the ability to decode. As much as I appreciate that whole language helps readers understand the beauty of a story, this is academic until children understand the relationship of letters and sounds to words. The research has born out that the only way to master reading is through phonics.

My answer to the question of whether we have, in the excessive placement of black boys in special education programs, a reading problem or a true special education problem may be answered as follows:

1. We can solve the problem by teaching children, particularly African American males, how to read.
2. The best way to teach children how to read is through phonics.
3. We should relax our age-grade expectations for all children, particularly boys and Black boys, and allow them to gradually learn how to read, with phonics being the first tool.

Special education is not a place but a service. If the reason for placement is due to a reading disorder, then the IEP must include a remedial reading curriculum to be taught by a reading specialist. In deference to the advocates of whole language, after boys have mastered phonics at their own maturation rate, reading assignments should consider their interests. On behalf of male students in America, I request that teachers include books on sports, adventure, automobiles, technology, science, horror, and mystery in their classroom libraries.

Boys tell me that reading materials in their classrooms are boring. When boys compare their assigned books to what they hear on the radio, e.g., rap music, or what they see on television, e.g., movies and sports, they have little desire to read. So besides emphasizing phonics and reading readiness, we must include interesting content in the learning-to-read mix.

A Reading or a Special Education Problem?

Reading Aloud

Teachers have been college trained and taught as children to believe that there is something magical and significant about having children read aloud. Like the written exam that has true-false or multiple-choice questions, reading aloud is seen as an efficient way of determining the reading ability of students.

For a left-brain reader, reading aloud is appropriate. But for right-brain, visual learners who create images as they read, reading aloud is not only difficult, but it slows them down. Reading aloud makes it difficult for them to create the mental images they need to comprehend and enjoy the text.

Other than in television broadcasting, what other professionals read aloud? I offer the research of Jeffery Freed to reinforce this point. In his book *Right Brain Children in a Left Brain World,* Freed discusses reading aloud:

Michael was typical of many right-brain and ADD children who find reading, particularly reading out loud, a tremendous source of frustration and embarrassment. They are faced with the challenge of seeing words, turning them into pictures in their heads, then verbalizing them. Because they tend to be more distracted and process the information more randomly, their eyes may jump ahead or behind the word they're supposed to be reading. The result is choppy, nonfluent reading. They may miss the little words, skip lines, and generally be poor oral readers. Yet these same children can be exceptional silent readers once they understand the concept of turning words into mental pictures.

While right-brain ADD children may have difficulty reading out loud, nature gives them a compensating strength from which to work: they can be excellent silent readers and speed readers. After all, their minds work visually and often at a feverish pace. It's fascinating to observe how the

61

most right-brain student, the child who flounders while reading out loud, is the one who is most likely to excel at silent reading. This is because reading is about comprehension, and comprehension is about visualization, the strength of the right-brain population.

The right brain child, however, is practically another species when it comes to reading. His style demands that he read quickly, scanning key words on the page in order to produce a detailed picture in his head. The right-brain child may eschew note taking, learning more effectively by skimming the text several times and visualizing the material. His memory bank becomes the notebook. His reading will give him a thumbnail sketch of the plot. Subsequent readings are like brushstrokes that fill in the vivid details. In many ways it can be said that under the ideal conditions, the right-brain child has a definite edge in reading comprehension because he visualizes so much better.

Keep in mind, however, that your right-brain child is, unfortunately, highly distractible, which works against visualization and comprehension. He doesn't have the left-brain sensibility to filter out noise, which is why in a busy classroom setting he often finds himself struggling to conjure up images and words on a page. All those distractions—the student sharpening his pencil, the note being passed, the second hand squeaking around the clock—are so much more interesting![23]

Rita Dunn's research explores the American "one size fits all" approach to reading and how it disdains allowing diversity, inclusion, and multiculturalism to drive pedagogy.

Some youngsters who read well are unable to extract much meaning from the printed word unless they hear the text being read. To illustrate, we found

A Reading or a Special Education Problem?

our daughter, Rana, reading aloud on the lawn in front of our home. When asked what she was, doing she replied, "I can only remember what I read when I hear the words." Since she had no one to read to and because she had heard that flowers might grow better when spoken to, she had decided to read to the flowers in order to have a reason for reading aloud.

Rana was correct about how she retains information. Although she reads well, she does not remember details that she sees in print unless she can also hear them. If she uses a tape recorder to learn information, she learns easily. When she must rely on books, either she or someone else must read the text aloud.

One day, when she was in the eighth grade, one of her teachers directed class to read a passage in the book and then to explain it in writing. As she read, Rana moved her lips and spoke words. The teacher asked her to read silently. She explained that she had difficulty understanding what she was reading unless she heard the words and asked if she might sit outside the room in the hall to read the information before she began to write the answers. The teacher responded in a derogatory manner, suggesting that if Rana could not understand a book without reading it aloud, she ought to obtain remedial assistance.

She did not understand that many youngsters are auditory rather than visual learners and that many are the reverse. Despite the teacher's unintentional discouragement, Rana's understanding and acceptance of the learning style has helped her to study and to learn through ways in which she can be successful. Had she not been aware, she might have had many more problems as a student. [24]

One child is placed in special education because he is expected to read by age five, six, or seven. Another child is placed because he was taught to read via whole language when he should have been taught phonics first. A right-brain learner is placed in special education because when reading aloud he has difficulty making the mental pictures he needs to understand the text. Lastly, a child who needs to hear the words is placed in special education because he has difficulty reading silently. Do we have a special education problem or a reading crisis in America?

In the next chapter, we will look further at the different learning styles of children. Teachers must realize that you do not teach the way you want to teach but the way children learn.

CHAPTER 6: LEARNING STYLES

What is the split-brain theory?
What percentage of your students are right-brain learners?
What percentage of your lesson plans are right brain?
What percentage of your tests are right brain?
What are five ways to teach a lesson? Which are left brain, and which are right brain?
When you were a student, what was your most memorable learning experience?
Was it a ditto sheet? A lecture? Reading a textbook? A hands-on discovery? A cooperative learning experience?

Once you ascertain the percentage of right-brain learners in your classroom, you will know how much right-brain instruction should be factored into your curriculum. This is the epitome of teaching the way children learn and not the way you want to teach.

Why don't teachers teach the way they themselves enjoy learning? I am confident that your most memorable learning experience was not with a ditto sheet, a textbook, or a lecture. Teaching will be much more effective and enjoyable for you and your students if you teach the way you like to learn.

Listed below is a simple survey of right- and left-brain strengths and challenges in learning. This will help you determine your children's learning styles (as well as your own). (R means right brain; L means left brain.)

1. R is not good at remembering names. L is not good at remembering faces.
2. R responds best to instruction by example. L responds best to verbal instructions.
3. R is able to express feelings and emotions freely. L is not easily able to express feelings and emotions.

4. R prefers classes where he/she studies or works on many things at once. L prefers classes where he/she has one assignment at a time.
5. R prefers multiple-choice tests. L prefers essay tests.
6. R is good at thinking up funny things to say and/or do. L is poor at thinking up funny things to say/or do.
7. R almost always can use whatever tools are available to get work done. L prefers working with proper materials.
8. R thinks best while lying flat on his/her back. L thinks best while sitting upright.
9. R is responsive to emotional aspects. L is responsive to logical verbal appeals.
10. R is skilled in showing by movement and action. L is skilled in giving verbal explanations.
11. R easily finds directions even in strange surroundings. L gets lost easily even in familiar surroundings.
12. R likes to be in noisy, crowded places where lots of things are happening. L likes to be in quiet settings where one can concentrate on a single activity to his/her best ability.

Jeffery Freed in his excellent book *Right Brain Children in a Left Brain World* offers the following learning style clues:

The more yes responses you have, the more to the right you or your child will be on this left-right brain continuum.

1. Is your child extremely wiggly?
2. Does your child have difficulty with coloring or handwriting?
3. Is your child extremely sensitive to criticism?
4. Is your child good with building toys, such as Lincoln Logs, Leggos, or Tinker Toys?
5. Is your child good at puzzles and mazes?
6. If you read a book to your child two or three times, is he or she capable of filling in missing words with almost perfect recall?
7. Is it extremely important that your child likes his or her teacher in order to do well in class?

Learning Styles

8. Is your child easily distracted, or does he daydream a lot?
9. Is your child unable to consistently finish tasks?
10. Does your child tend to act first and think later?
11. Is your child overwhelmed at sporting events, loud parties, amusement parks?
12. Does your child tend to shy away from hugs?
13. Does your child need constant reminders to do certain things?
14. Is your child extremely competitive and hates losing?
15. Does your child have a sense of humor?
16. Does he have a better than average ability to understand or create puns?
17. Is your child a perfectionist to the point that it gets in the way of trying new things?
18. Can your child recall a summer vacation or other event from one or two years ago in vivid detail?
19. When you are presented with a toy or a piece of furniture to assemble, are you likely to discard the printed directions and figure out how to build it yourself?
20. Are you better at thinking of ideas if you're left alone to concentrate rather than working in groups?
21. Do you rely mostly on pictures to remember things as opposed to names and words?
22. Do you have especially acute hearing?
23. When you are asked to spell a word, do you see it in your head rather than sound it out phonetically?
24. When you are studying a subject, do you prefer to get the big picture as opposed to learning a lot of facts?
25. Can you imagine things well in three dimensions?
26. Are you easily distracted to the point that you find yourself daydreaming a lot?
27. Are you good at hearing people out?
28. Do others tell you that you are good at reading people?
29. Is your handwriting below average or poor?[25]

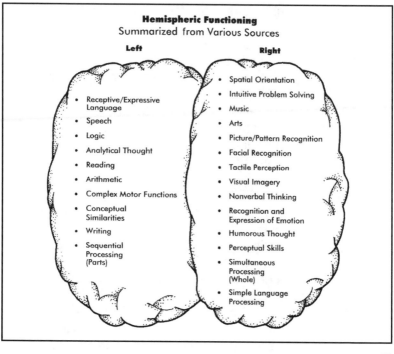

Hemispheric Functioning
Summarized from Various Sources

Left	Right
• Receptive/Expressive Language	• Spatial Orientation
• Speech	• Intuitive Problem Solving
• Logic	• Music
• Analytical Thought	• Arts
• Reading	• Picture/Pattern Recognition
• Arithmetic	• Facial Recognition
• Complex Motor Functions	• Tactile Perception
• Conceptual Similarities	• Visual Imagery
• Writing	• Nonverbal Thinking
• Sequential Processing (Parts)	• Recognition and Expression of Emotion
	• Humorous Thought
	• Perceptual Skills
	• Simultaneous Processing (Whole)
	• Simple Language Processing

26

The following chart by Rosalie Cohen[20] gives us even more information to better understand the contrast between left-brained and right-brained thinkers, between the analytical style and relational style.

Left-Brained Students	**Right-Brained Student**
As it is in general	As it could be
(Analytical)	(Relational)
Rules	Freedom
Standardization	Variation
Conformity	Creativity
Memory of specific facts	Memory for essence
Regularity	Novelty
Rigid order	Flexibility

Learning Styles

"Normality"	Uniqueness
Differences equal deficits	Sameness equals oppression
Preconceive	Improvise
Precision	Approximate
Logical	Psychological
Atomistic	Global
Egocentric	Sociocentric
Convergent	Divergent
Controlled	Expressive
Meanings are universal	Meanings are contextual
Direct	Indirect
Cognitive	Affective
Linear	Patterned
Mechanical	Humanistic
Unison	Individual in group
Hierarchical	Democratic
Isolation	Integration
Deductive	Inductive
Scheduled	Targets of opportunity

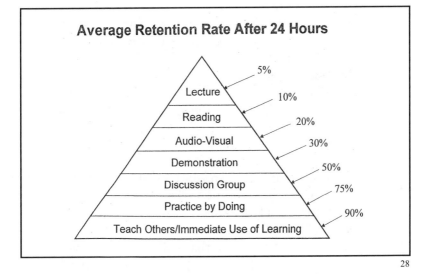

Average Retention Rate After 24 Hours

Lecture — 5%
Reading — 10%
Audio-Visual — 20%
Demonstration — 30%
Discussion Group — 50%
Practice by Doing — 75%
Teach Others/Immediate Use of Learning — 90%

28

KEEPING BLACK BOYS OUT OF SPECIAL EDUCATION

Dr. Howard Gardner believes that each child is 100 percent smart and that our total intelligence is made up of at least seven different types of smartness. This is in contrast to traditional IQ tests, which measure only language and math intelligence. Gardner's seven intelligences are as follows:

1. Linguistic learners
   - Word smart
   - Learns best through oral and written language
   - Hearing, saying, and seeing words
2. Logical, mathematical learners
   - Numbers smart
   - Learns best by categorizing, making own discovereries, classifying and working with abstract patterns and relationships
3. Spatial learners
   - Art smart
   - Learns best through visual presentations and by visualizing, using the mind's eye and working with colors, pictures
4. Body, kinesthetic learners
   - Body smart
   - Learns best through hands-on activities and by doing, touching, moving, and interacting with space
5. Musical learners
   - Music smart
   - Learns best through rhythm, music, and melody
6. Interpersonal learners
   - People smart
   - Learns best by sharing, relating, interacting, and cooperating with others
7. Intrapersonal learners
   - Self smart
   - Learns best by working alone, having self-paced instruction and individualized projects[29]

Learning Styles

I would like to add Howard Gardner's test to the litany of tests that were previously provided. Ideally, every IEP assessment should include Gardner's seven types of intelligence. Unfortunately, we have designed a school system that values only linguistic learners and logical mathematical learners. And even among those two categories, the linguistically inclined have far less chance of being placed in special education than mathematical, spatial, kinesthetic, musical, interpersonal, and intrapersonal learners. I wonder how many gifted and talented children are in special education classes in America today because of a misdiagnosis of learning and cognitive ability?

Jeffery Freed concurs with Howard Gardner and offers the following insight:

> Due to more than a decade of working one-on-one first with gifted and then with ADD children, I've had the framework to make a startling discovery: most gifted and virtually all children with ADD share the same learning style. Simply put, they are highly visual, nonsequential processors who learn by remembering the way things look and by taking words and turning them into mental pictures. The teaching techniques that work so well for gifted and talented children should also be used with ADD children. My hypothesis is that children who are labeled ADD fall on the right end of my continuum. This is the headline: children who are labeled with Attention Deficit Disorder are right brain, visual, and random in their processing.
>
> My premise is shared by psychologist Dr. George Dorry of Denver's Attention and Behavior Center, an expert on children and adults with ADD. I asked him one day if he had ever seen a child with ADD who was left brain and linear in his processing. Dorry's response: "It is the very nature of ADD to be distractible and nonlinear in one's thinking. The answer would have to be no."[30]

Bernice McCarthy has developed the 4Mat System. She believes there are four types of learners:

1. Innovative: Teachers need to create a reason for learning.
   Key question: why?
2. Analytic: Teachers need to give them the facts.
   Key question: what?
3. Common sense: Teachers need to let them try it.
   Key question: how?
4. Dynamic: Teachers need to let them teach themselves through discovery.
   Key question: what if?[31]

One of the most significant factors about right-brain learners is that they are what McCarthy describes as "innovative learners." Right-brain learners feel compelled to ask "why?" Why do I have to learn this? Why does this relate to my world, my community? These should be seen as excellent questions that display signs of critical thinking ability. Hitler's Germany and the Jones massacre occurred because the people involved did not think critically about what they were told to do. Like zombies, they simply obeyed, with disastrous outcomes.

If children have to stay in school from kindergarten through twelfth grade, 13 years, the least we can do is answer their most significant question: Why do I have to learn what you are teaching? It is not a belligerent or a defiant question. For right-brain students, it is an absolutely essential question that must be answered before real learning can take place. Until a right-brain learner is given an answer to this urgent question, there is little chance that motivational efforts and teaching expertise will be effective.

In his excellent book *The Pedagogy of the Oppressed*, Paulo Freire says that the ideal curriculum is one that addresses the needs of the community. To truly understand their students, teachers should walk the streets of the school neighborhood to get a better appreciation of the factors that exist there.

Learning Styles

Neighborhoods that are filled with liquor stores, crack houses, prostitution, drug dealers, and unemployment are, unfortunately, the realities that some students must deal with on a daily basis. Teachers should find creative ways to connect reading, math, science, and social studies to those realities. Both right- and left-brain learners will begin to understand and appreciate how school subjects relate to their daily lives.

For example, if the objective is to teach writing skills, then have students write letters to local council members, ministers, media, and judicial system officials to reconcile the relationship between crack and cocaine, which right now is a 100:1 ratio. Letters should be written to the police department about their "war on drugs." They can ask why, with 74 percent of all drug users being White, almost 70 percent of those convicted for possession are Black and Latino. If the police department does not know where the crack houses are in the neighborhood, students can anonymously let them know in their letters.

Unfortunately, teachers who function as custodians, referral agents, and instructors do not feel it is in their job description to answer students' urgent question, Why do I have to learn this? Fortunately, master teachers and coaches understand that until this question has been answered, education will be an exercise in futility.

In her book *Unicorns Are Real: A Right Brain Approach to Learning* Barbara Meister Vitale describes how some right-brain children, labeled as having severe, high-end motor coordination problems, had difficulty with puzzles.

I watched these kids. They were movers. They were up and down, in and out, and they'd rather draw pictures along the sides of the dittos than anything else. They were having a great time. They just couldn't put puzzles together. So I took the puzzle and put it together for one child. Then I had him take one piece at a time, move it to one side, and put it back in place again. He had no trouble. Next, I dumped the puzzle onto the desk, and he put it together beautifully. Why? Because I had shown him what it looked like when it was all put together.[32]

How remarkable! Right-brain learners need to see the big picture first. If you give them the big picture, if you let them know the learning agenda for the entire school day, you will be surprised and pleased at how well these learners perform. Left-brain learners think sequentially and in parts before they form their big picture. Right-brain learners need to see the whole picture first in order to understand the parts.

Only one of McCarthy's four types of learners (innovative, analytic, common sense, and dynamic) does well in American classrooms. Which one do you think it is? American schools gravitate toward the analytic learner. This learner is primarily left brain, and he or she wants teachers to give them the facts.

The other three types of learners (innovative, common sense, and dynamic) are not encouraged by most teachers and are often placed in special education. I wonder how many innovative learners we have in special education. I wonder how many common sense learners we have in special education. And I cannot begin to fathom how many dynamic learners and visionaries who are not restrained by the current standard and ask " what if?" are in special education.

Imhotep (the first doctor), Ahmose (the first mathematician), George Washington Carver, Lewis Latimer, Granville T. Woods, Charles Drew, Daniel Hale Williams, Ben Carson, and Mae Jamison were brilliant scholars who were driven by the question "what if?" I wonder how many dynamic students we have lost to special education because their learning style was not understood or appreciated.

Not only is our pedagogy geared toward left-brain learners, but our school day, from the intermediate grades on, is geared toward left-brain learning. The concept of departmentalization, where the school day is divided into seven to ten different periods and children go from one teacher to another, is geared toward the left-brain learner. Junior, middle, and senior high schools are organized in this way. Innovative, common sense, and dynamic learners

Learning Styles

want to ask, Is there any relationship between my first period math class and second period science class? my third period English class and fourth period social studies class? Right-brain learners are global, macro thinkers and look for the larger picture and relationships.

The impact of departmentalization on student-teacher relationships is tremendously negative. Research documents the need for junior, middle, and senior high schools to be smaller. They are beginning to realize that 5,000 students in a school is not good, even for left-brain learners. It is even more of a problem for right-brain learners. The mega-school is especially traumatic for students when they have a first period teacher who is a custodian, a second period referral agent, a third period instructor, a fourth period teacher, and a fifth period coach or master teacher.

Right-brain thinkers have a different view of time, as well, and cannot be restricted to learning a particular subject within the confines of a 45 to 50-minute period. In *Survival Strategies for Parenting Your ADD Child,* author George Lynn sheds the following light:

> Another example of this phenomenon would be the difficulty that an ADD child experiences in a classroom situation requiring him to make transitions from one activity to another. A normal kid can go through the change of focus required easily. I was doing X and now I'm doing Y. The ADD child looks up and continues to do X, becoming greatly distressed when his teacher tries to grind his gears to shift him to do Y.[33]

In *Teaching Teens with ADD and ADHD,* Chris Dendy provides the following chart to reinforce this concern:

Time Management Strategies	Left Brain Thinkers	Righ Brain Thinkers
Plan	What should be done? Develops a manageable list.	What could be done? Brainstorming occurs. To do list expands greatly.
Prioritize	List items in order of priority: important, next to important— 2, 3 or A, B, C.	Everything is important or it wouldn't be on the list. Can't pick just one. Priorities change quickly.
Schedule	Write dates and times on a calendar.	Can't decide which calendar to buy Must research all options. Writes notes and misplaces them and then loses the calendar.
Follow plan	Follow through is fun and is a reward in and of itself.	Once steps 1–3 are completed, the student becomes bored and weary; craves fresh ideas and new challenges. Joy and rewards come from producing new ideas and finding new challenges.[34]

Learning Styles

We could reduce the number of all children, particularly African American boys, in special education if we eliminated departmentalization and moved to smaller schools and classrooms.

Let me share with you how beautiful God's children are and the many different ways they learn. The following children never should have been placed in special education. Many of these children are gifted and simply have different learning styles. Consider the following anecdote:

> Ben looked around. He couldn't seem to follow the instructions that were printed on the sheet because they did not make sense to him. He turned to his neighbor Ed and asked what he was supposed to do after finishing the second problem. Before Ed could respond, the teacher called out impatiently, "The directions are printed for you. All you have to do is read them."

> Rita Dunn, in her excellent book *Teaching Students Through Their Individual Learning Styles,* reminds us that auditory students may need to hear instructions or directions. The printed word may not be effective for them.

> Susan smiled and played the tape again. Her fingers traced the words in the written script as she listened. She understood perfectly. For the first time reading was fun. After she finished the touching and feeling game with ease, she began to build the map with the pieces in the package. For the first time she enjoyed learning.[35]

> Many children are tactile, kinesthetic learners. They respond much better to touch. This reminds me of a story told by Thomas Armstrong in *The Myth of the ADD Child.*

A former third grade student could never sit still. While I demonstrated a lesson on the chalkboard, he had to poke the child sitting next to him or rock back and forth in his chair, distracting both me and the rest of the class.

I asked Tony if he would sponge off the art clay table while I presented a phonics lesson to the class. After the lesson I quizzed the class about the rules I had presented, the vowel blends, and Tony got a perfect score of 10. He had never received a score higher than three or four. [36]

Tony was a tactile, kinesthetic learner. Given the opportunity to touch, his learning ability improved tremendously. Why should he be placed in special education when he has the ability to learn like any other child?

Remember the ideal student? She is typically a left-brain learner. Have we become so rigid in American schools that we refer right-brain learners to special education because they do not have the left-brain attributes of the ideal student?

Jeffery Freed provides the following insight in the area of math:

I've worked with many a child who struggles with times tables, flops at flash cards, and fails to finish a set of problems as easy as 2+5. Yet only after a handful of tutoring sessions these right brain ADD children can be doing complex addition and multiplication problems (74x3 or 156+398) in their heads. The reason many bright students are failing in math is simply the way that it's taught, through drill, repetition, and timed tests. It's assumed that hearing math facts over and over again is the best way for all children to learn, but the truth is, this method only works for students who are left or whole brain. Traditional methods of teaching math bypassed the right brain child's greatest strength:

Learning Styles

the ability to access in whole images. Flash cards, it turns out, are fine if you take the "flash" out of them. They're visual, which helps children with a right brain learning style, but they're a nightmare for ADD kids because they demand quick processing, which is not congruent with their learning styles. Rush a visual learner and he's out of his game. Some schools understand this and they use "touch math" techniques, such as money counting, the abacus, and bead frames, which works infinitely better to illustrate math concepts for right brain kids than memorizing long lists of equations.[37]

Freed also adds interesting thoughts about handwriting:

Writing is almost without exception the most difficult subject for children with right brain learning styles to master. The right brain child will manifest problems with his writing from the first time he picks up a pen. His fine motor skills may be lagging during formative preschool years, so even learning the correct way to grip a pencil can be a formidable task. His multidimensional visual orientation also makes him more prone to errors in copying letters and numbers. He may reverse them or write entire words backwards. He has a difficult time bringing thoughts from his mental blackboard onto paper. It is very difficult for a right brain child to do more than one thing at a time.

As he struggles to translate pictures into words, form letters, spell, and punctuate, his mental picture becomes distorted. Even attempting to write his name can be an exercise in frustration. He hates to fail. His perfectionism keeps him from trying again. His teacher, however well meaning, may be correcting every little mistake rather than helping him build confidence and expressing himself. Left brain people think in symbols and words. So they experience very little difficulty in translating their thoughts onto paper. It is almost as if writing was developed for the left brain learner to learn.[38]

I wonder how many right-brain children, African American children and particularly African American males, have been placed in special education because they have poor penmanship, hand-writing skills, and difficulties writing cursive. I also wonder how many teachers expect Black boys to have this skill mastered as early as first or second grade and are comparing them to female students. I wonder how many boys write the correct answers but, because of poor penmanship, the teacher is unable to decipher the words.

Dr. Sydney Zentall, a professor of special education, comments:

> Our left brain schools teach spelling in black and white, usually using white chalk on a black board. So right brain children are going to be innovative and make liberal use of color. I found that color can capture the attention of children labeled ADD and improve their skills in copying written material. I also found that ADD children see letters and seem much more likely to pay attention if the letters are in color. I've been using this technique for the right brain and gifted children for years, and I can attest that color does make a difference.[39]

Do you like to read while sitting in an easy chair or at a desk, lying on a bed or on the floor? Students are expected to sit still from 9:00 a.m. to 3:00 p.m. on a hard chair, at a hard desk, keep quiet, and work independently—and they have to ask permission to move.

Have you ever let your students learn while sitting on something more comfortable than a hard chair? Many children, particularly right-brain children, are much better in a more comfortable position. I have observed numerous classrooms, and I love watching children who are immersed in learning while they are sitting on the floor with their legs folded or on a couch or in some other comfortable type of setting. Children really do learn in different ways.

Learning Styles

Not only is location important but also the time of day. Years ago, education professors told their students to teach reading and math early in the morning because they believed that was when students were most alert. That may not be totally true. Some youngsters perform at maximum capacity early in the morning while others do not seem to get started until late morning or midday. Efficient functioning varies greatly in children.

Remember when you were in college? Did you study in the morning or at night? Imagine having to study only at times dictated by your professor. If we really value children (and we say that education is for the children), we must appreciate that some children perform better in the morning and some in the afternoon. How unfortunate that some teachers will only test children in the morning although they are fully cognizant that many of their students perform far better in the afternoon.

I would also suggest that we seriously consider the best day of the week to test children. Unfortunately, for many of our children who live in violent neighborhoods, scheduling tests for early Monday morning after a traumatic weekend could be a disaster. Consider testing in the middle of the week and, with observation, determine whether morning or afternoon is better.

Unique factors to consider when teaching African American students:

- Teach historical events before and after 1619.
- Understand how most African Americans feel about good hair, pretty eyes, and lighter hue.
- Study Ebonics and learn code switching. In Black culture words are a figure of speech and are not to be taken literally.
- Black families are not monolithic (25 percent earn in excess $75,000; 42 percent earn $20,000 – $75,000; and 33 percent live below the poverty line).
- Understand why so many African American youth associate being smart with acting White.

- Place greater emphasis on sports and music.
- Recognize children with greater energy levels.
- Know that large numbers are right-brain learners.
  Be aware that there can be no significant learning until there is a significant student-teacher relationship.

Cooperative Learning

I am a strong advocate of cooperative learning. Research shows that the peer group has become the number one influence on our children. Peer pressure does not have to be negative. With cooperative learning, children can learn from each other. It is a humbling experience for teachers to observe students do a better job at teaching their peers.

For years teachers were the sole source of instruction in the classroom. When youngsters had difficulty acquiring knowledge, teachers believed that their charges had not paid attention. I wonder how much of that was driven by ego. Few realize that despite the quality of the teaching, some students are incapable of learning from an adult. These young people are uncomfortable when made to concentrate under the direction of an authority figure. They are fearful of failing, embarrassed to show an inability and, as a result, often become too tense to concentrate. For such students, either learning alone or with peers is an effective alternative to working directly with a teacher. In the end, it does not matter whether students learn from teachers or from each other.

Cooperative learning also can help bring the student-teacher ratio to a more effective, acceptable level. In many inner city schools, the student-teacher ratio exceeds 28 to 1. Research shows that the ideal ratio is 17 to 1. Few inner city schools possess that ratio.

After the peer group, the second greatest influence on children is rap music. Ironically, 70 percent of all rap music is purchased by White youth. Rap music is not only influential on African

Learning Styles

American children but on White children as well. It amazes me when teachers try to convince me that African American children cannot learn and should be placed in special education. Yet those same children can listen to a rap CD and in three to five minutes repeat the words verbatim. This is a tremendous skill. I challenge anyone reading this book to play a rap CD and in three to five minutes have it memorized.

If our children can memorize words from a rap CD, they can also remember the Constitution, the names of all 50 states, algebraic equations, and more. Children learn in different ways. The million-dollar question is, Can teachers put aside their ditto sheets, textbooks, and lectures and come up with new methods that incorporate the many different ways children learn? Most African American youth seem to possess selective auditory skills. Lectures bore them, but they can repeat rap songs lyric by lyric.

Since African American children, particularly African American males, have such a strong interest in rap music, let's use this interest in our pedagogy and curriculum. Consider using rap CDs rated PG and PG-13 in your classroom, and let the lyrics serve as the source of that week's vocabulary words and social studies project. Set multiplication tables and anything else that children must memorize to rap music.

Teachers do not need to do this themselves. Have students develop their own Constitution rap, 50-states rap, and multiplication tables rap. Let that boy who is always beating his desk put words to the rap. Your students will love it.

I suggested this idea to some teachers. They said they gave their students an assignment and putting the concept to rap was optional. The students were resistant. Several ideas came to mind when I heard this. The problem was that the teachers had not convinced themselves that this was a good way to teach the concept. If they had, they would not have made this assignment optional.

I asked, "Are homework assignments optional? Are taking tests optional? Then why would you make the rap approach optional?" Also, students may have resisted because the concept was boring and irrelevant, and they had not been convinced it was important enough to learn. If teachers had explained the significance and relevance of the concept, the children might have been more eager to do the rap assignment.

Teachers often try to convince me that children have poor communication and verbal skills and are not auditory learners. When I point out that they are able to memorize a rap CD just by listening to it, most teachers will begin to see the light. Before saying that children have weak verbal, communication, and auditory skills, teachers should look at the content of the information being disseminated. The students (particularly African American males) may not have poor communication skills. It could be that the subject of the lecture and the lecture approach are boring.

I encourage all teachers to develop learning centers in their classrooms. It is unfortunate and arrogant to assume that all students will master concepts with a ditto sheet or a textbook. Children learn in many ways, including writing, oral expression, pictures, fine arts, and artifacts. Each learning center should be focused on one of those ways.

For example, in the writing center, children can read books and magazine articles about a particular concept. They could then move (yes, I said move) from the writing center to the oral center, where there would be cassette and CD players. Children could listen to speeches by Dr. King, Malcolm X, or even books-on-tape. Next, they would move to the visual or picture center where they could view pictures illustrating the concept. In the artifacts learning center (tactile, kinesthetic), children could touch and feel artifacts related to the concept that is being taught. In the fine arts learning center, they might develop a play or they could hear a song or dramatic production about the idea. This reinforces Gardner's concept of seven styles of intelligence.

Learning Styles

I have advocated learning centers for years, and I understand the challenges. Many of our schools, especially in the inner city, were built in the early 1900s. Desks do not move and there is limited room, so it is difficult to develop learning centers. Also, some teachers simply do not like a lot of movement in their classrooms.

Let me share a secret with you. Children, especially right-brain children and African American children, particularly African American boys, can learn while moving. Some teachers are concerned about the increased noise level when children move about the room. But children can also learn when there are higher noise levels, especially right-brain learners.

Another challenge to developing learning centers is the lack of financial resources and the additional work required. Many teachers have actually said, "You want me to develop five different lessons for one concept?" The answer is an emphatic yes. If we do not expand the pedagogy and realize that children learn in different ways, excessive special education placements will continue to increase.

There are other ways to be more inclusive in your teaching. For example, try and go all day Monday without using a ditto sheet. Have you ever seen an addict go through withdrawal? It is not unlike a teacher with no ditto sheet. Also, try going all day Wednesday without using a textbook, or all day Friday without lecturing. Children learn in different ways. Let's try something different next Monday, Wednesday, and Friday.

Teachers often ask children to read an assignment and then write about what they just read. That is purely a left-brain project: read and write. Why not have students read the information and then draw it, create a dramatic production, or put it to rap?

I want to emphasize drawing because many professionals with BAs, MAs, and PhDs still draw using stick figures. Could the reason be that from fourth grade on, most American schools offer little drawing and fine arts? I would like you to draw yourself, and then you will appreciate the point that I'm trying to make. Though we are mature, adult professionals, our artistic skills are totally underdeveloped. And that may explain our reluctance to have students draw, set concepts to music, etc.

Finally, for the rest of the day, act as if you are left-handed. Experience what it is like being left-handed in our left-brain, right-handed country. Experience what it is like to sit at a desk as a left-handed person, turn a doorknob with your left hand, or operate the toilet with your left hand and you will better appreciate what it is like for right-brain children and left-handed people to live in a left-brain, right-handed world.

In the next chapter, we will look at the different ways in which boys and girls learn. This will help us to further understand why there are so many African American males in special education and even why there are more White males in special education than White females. This is more than a race issue. There is a gender issue that also needs to be resolved.

CHAPTER 7: GENDER LEARNING DIFFERENCES

Understanding how boys and girls learn differently may be the most important issue in this book. With such a disproportionate percentage of males placed in special education—almost a two-to-one ratio between White males and White females and almost a four-to-one ratio between African American males and African American females—it is obvious that in America we have not fully understood male learning styles and gender differences.

In my workshops for teachers I always ask the following questions:

1. Did you know that boys and girls are different? Invariably, teachers will say yes, they know boys and girls are different.
2. When teaching a classroom of boys and girls, how do you allow for those differences?
3. Have you ever taken a course in male learning styles? Have you ever taken a course in African American male learning styles?
4. What are some of the differences in the ways boys and girls learn?
5. What gender differences in behavior and cognitive ability affect learning?

Listed below are some general characteristics of boys that differentiate them from girls:

- More aggressive
- Higher energy level
- Shorter attention span
- Slower maturation rate
- Less cooperative
- Physically larger
- Influenced more by peer group
- Greater interest in math than reading

- Gross motor skills more developed than fine motor skills
- Not as neat as girls
- Louder
- Distinctive walk
- Larger, more sensitive ego
- Hearing inferior to that of girls

If we know that boys are more aggressive than girls, how do we allow for that difference in the classroom?

If we know that boys have a shorter attention span, what should we do differently in constructing our lesson plans?

If we know that boys mature more slowly than girls, how do we respond to that difference in our classrooms?

If we know that boys are more competitive and less co-operative, how does that change our pedagogy?

If we know that boys are more influenced by their peer group, do we handle them differently around their peers?

How do we allow for the fact that boys are more advanced in gross motor skills and girls are more advanced in fine motor skills?

If we know that, on average, boys are not as neat as girls, do we allow for any differences in their notebook organizational skills?

If we know that boys have larger and more sensitive egos, how do we relate to their personality?

If we know that girls hear better than boys, do we make classroom seating adjustments?

It is not enough to theoretically know that boys and girls are different and not allow for those differences. If we are cognizant of gender differences, it is incumbent upon us to make the necessary adjustments (other than disproportionately placing of males of all races and ethnic groups in special education).

Whether gender differences are genetic or caused by environment factors (family upbringing, socioeconomic status, etc.) is being hotly debated and researched across many disciplines, including education. What do you think? Are gender learning differences due to nature or nurture? How much is genetic and how much is cultural?

Gender Learning Differences

Brain Gender Differences

Part of Brain	Function	Similarities and Differences	Impact
Arcuate fasciculus	Curving bundle of nerve fibers in the central nervous system	Likely develops earlier in girls as evidenced by their earlier speed capabilities	Females speak in sentences earlier than males
Broca's Area	Motor area for speech process; grammatical structure for word production	More highly active in females	Improved verbal communication skills in females
Cerebellum and Corpus Callosum	Contains neurons that connect to other parts of the brain and spinal cord; connects the two hemispheres of the brain	Larger in females	Females have superior language and fine motor skills; helps females coordinate the two sides of the brain better
Cerebral Cortex	Contains neurons that promote highly intellectual functions and memory; interprets sensory impulses	Thicker in males on the right side of the brain; thicker in females on the left side	Males tend to be right brain dominant; females tend to be left brain dominant
Estrogen	Several female sex hormones that shape female brain	Much more present in females than males	In females, lowers aggression, competition
Testosterone	Male steroid sex hormone	Much more present and functional in males	Increases aggression and competition

40

89

An excellent article by Dr. Francis Wardle, "The Challenge of Boys in Our Early Childhood Programs," cites the following:

> **Physical activity.** In general, boys are more physical than girls. Far more boys engage in rough and tumble play than do girls. Boys also tend to enjoy physical activity on the playground, which is also cultural, as men in our culture engage in physical sports. Our boys need for more physical activities is probably due to culture. It is neurological as well. The brains of boys develop slower than those of girls, even before birth. Further, on average, boys tend to be more aggressive than girls, a trend that appears in many cultures. Not only is this due to brain development, but also due to male sex hormones.
>
> **Space.** Boys simply take up more space than girls in their daily activities, both indoors and out. From the teacher's perspective they seem to spread out, use the far reaches of the playground, want to push the limits on field trips. Maybe this is one reason boys love to play and work on the floor.
>
> Kinesthetic learning. Learn through movement. Boys seem to thrive using kinesthetic learning, which fits well with the use of space needs for physical activity and their aggressive behavior. They love outdoor projects, gardens, building with units and hollow blocks, field trips and games.
>
> Hands-on learning. Boys are more advanced than girls in mathematical reasoning, spatial ability, and mechanical ability while girls score higher on memory, perceptual accuracy, verbal fluency, and language tasks.[41]

Janice Hale further explains why there may be a greater number of Black boys in special education, more than even White males. She offers the following:

Gender Learning Differences

African American children are generally more kinesthetic than White children and have a higher level of motor activity. There is also medical evidence that African American males have a higher testosterone level than White males (Loscocco 1994). African American children, particularly boys, should not be required to sit for long periods of time without an opportunity to spend energy.[42]

In my book *Countering the Conspiracy to Destroy Black Boys,* I use the following graph to measure attention span:

HYPERACTIVITY: A Diagnosis in Search of a Patient

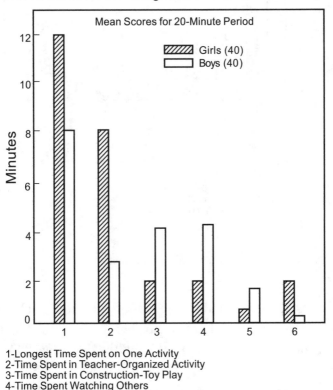

1-Longest Time Spent on One Activity
2-Time Spent in Teacher-Organized Activity
3-Time Spent in Construction-Toy Play
4-Time Spent Watching Others
5-Longest Time Watching Others
6-Time Spent Painting Alone

Diane McGuinnes, *When Children Don't Learn*

91

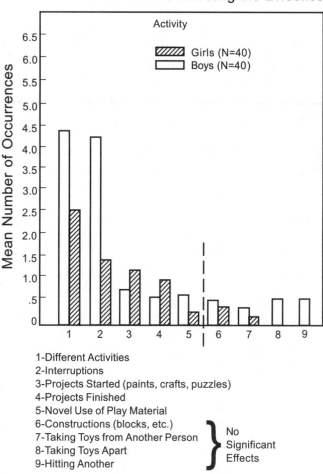

HYPERACTIVITY: Unraveling the Evidence

1-Different Activities
2-Interruptions
3-Projects Started (paints, crafts, puzzles)
4-Projects Finished
5-Novel Use of Play Material
6-Constructions (blocks, etc.)
7-Taking Toys from Another Person
8-Taking Toys Apart
9-Hitting Another

} No Significant Effects

Diane McGuinnes, *When Children Don't Learn*

A psychologist and I were walking through a school and she commented, "Which boy is just being a boy and which one is ADD or ADHD, because I can't tell the difference?" What a profound observation! They were just being boys. So help me understand, she queried, which one is just a boy and which one is afflicted with ADD or ADHD?

Gender Learning Differences

I never will forget the kindergarten boy who, after his first week, told me in frustration, "You can't do anything in this class." He felt totally restricted in a classroom designed for females. He was looking for briefcases and hard hats and hammers and balls and trucks, but there were none of those things. Flabbergasted, he said, "You can't do anything in this class."

In an hour-long class, boys' attention span will average about 8 minutes; some researchers say 22 minutes. What are the consequences of giving a 30 to 50-minute lesson to a student with an 8 to 22-minute attention span? Should boys be placed in special education because the lesson plan is too long, or should the teacher shorten the lesson plan to make it more commensurate with the children's learning style?

If we know that boys have a shorter attention span because they produce less serotonin and that this is genetically driven, why are we trying to force boys to increase their attention span? If you must use a longer lesson plan, then compromise by making the curriculum more relevant and reducing the use of ditto sheets and textbooks. When boys study subjects that interest them—sports, adventure, technology, automobiles, etc.—their attention span increases.

What can we learn from the fact that boys mature slower than girls? From kindergarten through twelfth grade, there is almost a three-year difference. Earlier I mentioned that some schools are experimenting with putting eight-year-old boys in classes with six-year-old girls. In many European countries, including Germany, Switzerland, Belgium, and Hungary, the entrance of boys into elementary school is delayed until age six or seven. Unfortunately, in America parents use school as a babysitting service, so I am not suggesting that we delay the entrance of boys until age six or seven because many parents would not know what to do with their sons until that age.

Maturation differences between boys and girls are expressed in many ways. Schools do not value how well boys can hold and manipulate big toys such as trucks and balls. They do value fine motor skills, such as the ability to manipulate pencils, pens, and crayons. Unfortunately, many schools expect five- and six-year-old boys to have the same level of penmanship as five- and six-year-old girls. Boys who are unable to write or color as well as girls are threatened with special education.

If we know that girls hear three times better than boys, teachers should change their seating charts and put boys in the front of the class. Let me also explain why boys talk louder (beyond the testosterone issue) and respond better to a strong voice. In the excellent book *Equity in the Classroom,* edited by Patricia Murphy, the following insight is provided:

> Males tend to extract information from context while females tend to pay attention to context in a study of a problem.

- In considering male reasoning or other male problem solving, males tend to take analytical-rule-based approaches while females tend to take holistic approaches and emphasize empathy.
- Males tend to be more hasty, impulsive, and willing to take risks while females exercise more care and deliberation.
- Males tend to attribute success to their own efforts and failure to external factors while females do the reverse. The perception of personal failure may inhibit subsequent performance.
- Interactions among males, including their discourse, are marked by competition while females appear to prefer to work in cooperation. Their discourse is relational, the reference made to the previous speaker.
- Girls work in a concentrated way. Subject matter is worked through in half the time used by boys.

Gender Learning Differences

- Girls are well prepared.
- Girls keep strictly to the subject.
- Girls see the lesson as a shared venture.
- Girls listen and show respect when others speak.
- Girls are helpful to each other.
- Boys are active in an anarchistic way.
- Boys have a low degree of preparation.
- Boys broaden subjects and include new angles and points of view.
- Boys see the lesson as an individual matter.
- Boys constantly interrupt each other.
- Boys compete with each other in getting the teacher's attention.[44]

Before we continue, I am in no way suggesting that these differences are 100 percent universal. Not all boys are aggressive, have shorter attention spans, show slower maturation rates, exhibit more advanced gross motor skills, are less verbal, or can't hear as well as girls. But on average these are some of the gender differences. More importantly, it is obvious from the disproportionate percentage of boys, particularly African American males, in special education that teachers respond to these differences. Being different is not synonymous with being deficient. Boys and girls simply are different. Boys and girls each have unique strengths and unique challenges to deal with.

To serve boys in the classroom, teachers must be aware of and understand gender learning differences. Teachers must allow and make adjustments for those differences without resorting to putting boys in special education.

Boys have larger and more sensitive egos than girls. Boys with ADD or ADHD tend to be more oppositional and aggressive than girls and thus are more of a discipline problem. While 67 percent of boys with ADHD are diagnosed to have Oppositional Defiance Disorder (ODD), only 33 percent of girls are so labeled.

Boys possess a greater propensity for rebelling against authority and engaging in conflict than girls, who are more likely to comply with hierarchical structure. The oppositional style of boys is seen as early as kindergarten and stands in contrast to young females who tend to avoid conflict and preserve harmony. In the book *Bad Boys,* Ann Ferguson makes the following observations:

> African American boys are not accorded the masculine dispensation of being naturally "naughty." Instead, the school reads their expression and display of masculine naughtiness as a sign of an inherent injudicious, insubordinate nature that as a threat to order must be controlled. Consequently, school adults view any display of masculine mettle on the part of these boys, through body language or verbal rejoinders, as a sign of insubordination.
>
> In confrontation with adults, what is required from them is a performance of absolute passivity that goes against the grain of masculinity. Black boys are expected to internalize the ritual obeisance in such exchanges so that the performance of docility appears to come naturally. This is not a lesson that all children are required to learn, however. The disciplining of the body within school rules has specific race and gender overtones. For Black boys the enactment of docility is a preparation for adult racialized survival rituals of which the African American adults in the school are especially cognizant. For African American boys, bodily forms of expressiveness have repercussions in the world outside the chain linked fence of the school. The body must be taught to endure humiliation in preparation for future enactments of submission.[45]

Russell Skiba discusses this in *The Color of Discipline.* African American males tend to be viewed through highly subjective lenses tinted by biased attitudes. Often African American males are suspended, placed in special education, or expelled because of a look, a shrug of the shoulders, a type of walk, or the failure to quickly jump to attention. Some schools believe that the best way to teach the Black male is to follow the military formula—break him down and then build him up. If we understand the male ego, which is large and sensitive, such treatment is not in the interest of educating our boys.

Boys have gone from kindergarten through eighth grade without experiencing a Black male teacher. Many schools do not have one Black adult male in the building. If a Black male is present, he is usually a maintenance engineer first, a security guard second, a physical education teacher third, an administrator fourth (some schools may actually hire Black men as assistant principals, which is equivalent to being in charge of all the "bad" Black boys), and a classroom teacher last.

There is a power struggle going on in many schools between Black boys and female teachers. In the primary grades, teachers can use their size to discipline students, but from the fourth grade on, as boys become bigger, they become threatening and intimidating. Furthermore, many Black boys do not have a father in the home. Presently only 32 percent of our youth have their fathers present. As a result, there is not only a desire of many educators to break the Black boy down but there is also a counter-struggle by Black boys to take teachers on one-on-one. In *Countering the Conspiracy to Destroy Black Boys,* I call this the "showdown," and it is similar to a rite of passage.

When the showdown begins, these are some of the potential outcomes:

1. The female teacher, out of emotional control, hollers at the child. The class laughs. Willie sits down slowly, causing further disruption. The class, Willie, and probably the teacher know Willie won this battle.

2. The female teacher responds inconsistently to Willie's behavior. He wins because she never reproved his negative behavior in the past. If her response is unassertive, he also wins.

3. The female teacher sends Willie downstairs to the principal's office. Probable actions include suspension, special education placement, and expulsion. Willie wins against the female teacher because she was incapable of handling the situation herself. He may lose to the principal or special education teacher, but he did not lose to her.

4. The female teacher sends Willie to the corner outside the classroom door. This showdown is a draw. The battle has been delayed indefinitely.

5. The female teacher assertively and consistently tells Willie to go to his seat and he complies. The female teacher wins this encounter.[46]

The good news is that most boys subconsciously want their female teachers to win the showdown. They want someone to show their concern about them. But if a teacher shows fear, she will never be effective with Black male students.

Winning a showdown is not based on gender or size. I know too many five-feet-tall women in their 60s with six-feet sons in their 20s who say, "I brought you in here, and I will take you out." Boys know which teachers are afraid of them, disrespect them, and have low respect for themselves. They know they can easily manipulate classroom situations with such teachers. Boys also know which teachers care about them, are fearless around them, and respect themselves.

One of the important lessons to learn about Black male culture and the Black male ego is that you must never embarrass a boy in front of his peer group. The peer group is all-important. Peer influence combined with a large ego can form

Gender Learning Differences

a fortress against effective communication. You cannot win against an inflated ego and friends egging him on. Showing the child respect, even during an angry showdown, will be more effective than trying to humiliate him in front of his peers. Better to understand, respect, and work with the dynamics to quickly restore order to the classroom. Following are ways to deal with the showdown and maintain your authority in the classroom.

- Show immediate respect by calling the boy by his last name, e.g., "Mr. Johnson" or even "Scholar Johnson."
- Refrain from fussing too much and asking a lot of questions. Boys tell me all the time that their female teachers and mothers often talk too much when disciplining them. As a result, they tune them out. Make your statement clear, straight, and to the point. Do not ask questions like, "Why did you do that?" Why is irrelevant, and often children do not know why they behaved in a certain way. Make your expectations for good behavior clear.
- Preface your discipline statement with a positive statement, such as "You're smart," "You're strong," or "You're usually a leader in the classroom." This will help him save face in front of his peers. It will also let him know that you are not just trying to beat him down and that you recognize his strengths and abilities despite the unacceptable behavior.
- Enforce male and female discipline fairly and consistently. Do not let girls get away with behaviors that boys are often punished for. Do not give chance after chance.
- The secret to winning the showdown is maintaining eye contact and a strong tone of voice. This conveys self-respect and establishes your authority.
- Pick your battles. Now that you are learning about innate male behaviors, pick and choose which behaviors constitute true offenses and which are just silliness or male "posturing."
- Do not take yourself too seriously. If your boys see that you have a sense of humor, some of the tension may be alleviated. This also lets them know that you care about them.

If you are wrong, do not hesitate to say "I'm sorry." This model of humility can be used as a teachable moment for boys who often find it difficult, because of peer influence and inflated egos, to admit they are wrong.

In the book *Gender and Education,* the author describes some of the innocence lost by boys:

> Boys are born with the same emotional potential as girls. Boys have faces as expressive as girls do. Boy babies cry more. There is every reason to believe that boys have as much neurological potential for an emotional life as do girls. But something gets lost in boys and as somebody who has worked in elementary and secondary schools all of my professional career, I can tell you, you can watch the loss of facial expressions in boys as they turn into men.
>
> We know that by kindergarten a girl is six times more likely to use the word love than a boy. By the time the boys are eight or nine years of age, mothers routinely report to me that they can no longer read their boys' faces as they used to, that they have gone somehow "stony." A teacher asked me the other day, "What is it that happens to boys in third grade? They're so open and innocent up until then and then we lose them."
>
> By the age of eight or nine, a boy is measuring everything he does on one dimension, from strong to weak. If you want to understand boy psychology, they put everything through the strong-weak filter. This keeps a boy locked up because he may not be able to articulate his experience and he may be ashamed that he can't. If he knows he can articulate it and he's ashamed that he can't, then the best course, the strongest looking course, is to be silent.[47]

Gender Learning Differences

Teachers need sensitivity training to better understand African American male students and their biases toward these children. We want to break Black boys down, yet we want them to be verbally expressive and emotional. You cannot have it both ways, especially as his experiences are being filtered through this strong-weak psychology.

In *Gender and Education,* the following conversation with boys on this issue is recounted:

Is it difficult for boys to have all women teachers? "They're pretty used to it," he says of boys. Is it easier for boys to have men teachers? "Yeah, they understand us more or something. They understand what we're trying to say." What do women have trouble understanding about boys? "They don't like to be gotten mad at." Allen makes a simple point, that boys don't like being yelled at, yet that makes up a large part of their lives. I'm reminded of a librarian, a woman who lamented once, "Adults feel justified in yelling at boys because they are so bad all the time." The assumption is that yelling helps, especially in communicating dissatisfaction to boys and that boys don't suffer from it as much as girls might. This is not my experience. Boys typically don't show that they suffer from yelling, because being a boy requires that they not show it, but it hurts.[48]

Teachers need to be aware that this angry, stony-faced, six-foot-three, 14-size-shoe Black male with a scowl on his face is, in his inner core, a youngster who wants to be hugged, smiled at, and encouraged. Children who cause the most disciplinary problems need the most attention—affection, hugs, words of encouragement, and smiles. Boys say they do not experience these things from their teachers. In sum, there is a conflict between school culture and Black male culture.

School Culture	Black Male Culture
I	We
Individualism	Collectivity
Competition	Cooperation
Academics	Sports/Rap
Report infractions to an authority figure	Self-defense

It is challenging for African American males to navigate their way through the maze of school culture while still maintaining a position of strength in Black male culture. It is a given that parents, schools, and the society at large want them to do well academically—and so do they. But, for example, when a Black boy is recommended for advanced placement, honors, or gifted and talented class, this presents an unusual problem for him. If he takes advantage of this opportunity, he must spend less time with his peer group. Schools underestimate the importance to Black boys of the peer group bond. Schools that have been more effective in this area have created ways for African American males to advance and still remain bonded to the peer group through strategies such as cooperative learning, greater Black advance placement representation, role model programs, counseling, and the Minority Student Achievement Network.

It would be suicidal for a boy to be in advanced classes if he cannot continue to play basketball, fight, and rap because that is what the Black peer culture values. Educators need to understand this tension between Black male culture and school culture.

As I described at length in *To Be Popular or Smart: The Black Peer Group,* in some circles Black boys are accused of being gay and acting White if they participate in advanced classes. I am reminded of the movie in which a Black male college student feels he must take an advanced math class in secret. He did not want his peers to think something was wrong with him because he loved math and wanted to be further challenged by the advanced class.

Another cultural conflict is in the area of fighting. In Black male culture, self-defense is critical. Yet schools say if someone hits you, tell an authority. Within Black male culture and street culture, males must hit back. They must take care of their "business" themselves. In fact, their parents tell them that if someone hits them to strike back. I have known parents to tell their sons that if they do not fight back, they will have to face a beating when they got home. That puts the boy between the proverbial rock and hard place, but such is the life of Black boys. Rather than face the wrath of a parent, they would rather take (or give) their punishment on the street. Teachers and administrators must understand how thoroughly entrenched self-defense is in Black male culture.

The following passage describes how many Black boys feel about their need to defend themselves and their school's lack of will:

One of the big issues that pulls us all together is juvenile vigilantism, which is boys' adaptation to a situation in which their need to be strong seems to be threatened by the lack of adult strength and their environment. A boy in Michigan said to me, "If I join a gang I am 50 percent safe. If I don't join a gang I am zero percent safe." The bottom line is he doesn't see that aligning himself, allowing his aggression and his need for power to be channeled into pro-social, adult agendas, is likely to meet his basic need of safety. When I asked a nine-year-old boy from a dangerous neighborhood in California what would it take to make him feel safer here, the only answer he could come up with was, "If I had a gun of my own."

One 16-year-old boy we interviewed in our prison project pointed very specifically to one day at age eight, that he understands now to be the turning point in his life. He says he was in third grade, on the schoolyard, when one of his friends was jumped by a bunch of older boys, fourth graders. He said the teacher turned her back and went inside. In that moment he realized that he was on his own out there, filled with the essential priority of being safe and being strong. Given that adults are not going to help that, obviously, you are on your own, and a lot of very dangerous things happen because of that.[49]

For many of our boys, their greatest challenge is not passing algebra, geometry, trigonometry, biology, chemistry, or physics. It is the four- to eight-block walk from home to school. It is trying to be safe on school playgrounds while teachers and administrators turn a blind eye. It is trying to negotiate a system that they perceive to be antithetical to their growth and development.

Departmentalization has created a huge problem in the area of student-teacher relationships. It is difficult for African American youth to move every 45 minutes from one teacher to the next and maintain the all-important bond. It is even more difficult for African American students to adjust to having a first period custodian, a second period referral agent, a third period instructor, a fourth period teacher, and a fifth period coach. (See Chapter 4 for a discussion of these sobriquets.) Of course, if we discard departmentalization, we risk some students ending up with a custodian for the entire school day. The main issue I want to stress here is that that African American students have a difficult time adjusting to new teachers every 45 minutes.

Gender Learning Differences

Earlier we mentioned that many African American students divide teachers into two categories: those who fear them and those who do not. In *Other People's Children,* Lisa Delpit describes the differences in teachers' communication styles and the confusion this can cause. Some teachers can effectively handle the majority of problems that arise by themselves. Other teachers frequently send children to the office for disobeying their directives. Parents are called in for conferences. The parents' response is usually the same: "They do what I say. If you just tell them what to do, they'll do it. I tell them at home that they have to listen to what you say."

Black children expect an authority figure to act with authority. When the teacher acts like a "chump," the message is sent that this adult has no authority, and the children react accordingly. In other words, the students believe that an authoritative person gets to be a teacher because she is authoritative. In contrast, some members of the middleclass expect one to achieve authority by the acquisition of an authoritative role. That is, the teacher is the authority because she is the teacher.

As Ruby Payne would suggest, that is not going to work with African American students who may laugh when disciplined. This can truly irritate an adult, but it is simply another self-defense mechanism of African American students as they respond to what they feel is a conflict between the values of the school and their own culture.

The most important subject for African American children to master is reading. This is not only an individual issue but also a social one. More than 90 percent of inmates enter prison illiterate. Ironically, many inmates who learn how to read in prison read more than people who are "free." How unfortunate it is that they had to become incarcerated to experience the beauty of reading.

Peer Groups

Parents and teachers may be doing their best, but if the Black peer group has not been factored into the picture, their efforts may not be effective. In *To Be Popular or Smart: The Black Peer Group,* I describe abysmal situations where African American students are doing well in school and, as a result, are teased by their peer group. Peer groups strip males of their masculinity, and African American students are accused of acting White.

As Beverly Tatum wrote in her book *Why Are Black Kids Sitting Together in the Cafeteria?* Black children feel that school, especially an integrated school, is an alien place and that the only time they can relax is with each other in the cafeteria. Ironically, when White students sit together in the cafeteria, that is not questioned, but because the onus of race is placed on Black students, we have to defend why they are sitting together.

If we are to educate African American students well, we must infiltrate the power of peer pressure, the number one influence on African American youth. It is naive for educators to attempt to educate African American students when the Black peer group does not value academic achievement. Our problems could be greatly reduced if we found creative ways to convince the Black peer group to value such achievement.

There are many reasons for this phenomenon. In my book *Solutions for Black America,* I discuss post-traumatic slavery disorder in more detail from a psychological perspective. I also recommend that you read the work of John Ogbu, who describes the social dynamics of minority groups. Minority groups fall into two major classifications: involuntary and voluntary. Involuntary minority groups are those who become incorporated into a nation through conquest, slavery, or colonization. Voluntary minority groups are those who become incorporated into a nation through voluntary emigration. Involuntary groups tend to oppose the cultural values of the majority in order to keep the conquerors, slavers, and colonizers from wiping out their indigenous culture. They feel they cannot adopt any of the ways of the majority without giving up parts of their own culture.

Voluntary minorities differ in that the societies into which they immigrate generally tolerate their culture. African Americans (through slavery), Native Americans (through conquest), and to some extent Mexican Americans (through conquest of the U.S. Southwest) are classified as involuntary minorities.

Involuntary minorities see schools as majority institutions. Therefore academic achievement challenges their group loyalty and ethnic identities. Voluntary minorities are secure in their ethnic identities, but they want to learn new ways that will enable them to succeed in their new country. For them, schooling is a new path that leads to opportunity.

Asian Americans constitute voluntary minorities. They use schooling as a path to achievement in the broader society. Unlike the experience of involuntary minorities, the dominant culture does not try to eradicate the culture and language of voluntary immigrants.

Instilling a Positive Mindset

How do we change students' mindsets? It is difficult for Black ideology to change if African American students are in school buildings with few African American teachers. Role modeling is significant, and it is difficult for African Americans to strive to be engineers, doctors, computer programmers, and accountants when they are exposed to so few professionals in those areas versus the high-visibility African Americans they are exposed to in sports and music.

On a weekly or monthly basis, consider inviting a positive-role-model African American male into the school building. Ideally he should work in a math- or science-related field.

Teach African American history year round. Currently, African American history has been confined to the shortest month of the year and taught incorrectly. It is understandable why so many African American youth associate being smart with being White when their history begins in slavery and is only taught 28 days out of 365.

We can change the negative mindset of African American youth if their history is taught throughout the year and if the lessons begin with the pyramids and not the plantations. Unfortunately, most teachers, including African American teachers, know more history post-1619 than pre-1619. African American children who are taught that Imhotep, not Hippocrates, was the father of medicine never associate being smart with acting White. People who have a solid understanding of their history do not make such asinine statements.

Ruby Payne analyzes this dynamic from a different perspective, that of poverty.

Another example of a poverty characteristic is an incident at church, where a lady receives money and is immediately besieged with requests. One of the hidden rules of poverty is that any extra money is shared. Middleclass puts a great deal of emphasis on being self-sufficient. In poverty, the clear understanding is that one will never get ahead so when extra money is available it is shared or immediately spent. There are always emergencies and needs. One might as well enjoy the money. She will share the money. She has no choice. If she does not, the next time she is in need, she will be left in the cold. It is the hidden rule of the support system. In poverty, people are possessions and people can rely only on each other. It is absolutely imperative that the needs of the individual come first. After all, that is all you have, people.[50]

Gender Learning Differences

When I read this quote, I immediately thought of the famous religious philosopher, Mbiti, and the African proverb, "I am because we are." Beyond the issue of poverty, we must uncover what it is about our culture and value system that makes people believe "I have mine and you have yours to get." In the classroom that means, "I have 100, you have 40, tough luck for you." On the other hand, as some teachers have been known to say, "I've got mine."

We should not be teaching our children these values. Children who have an African frame of reference enter the classroom with a desire to do things together. It is an alien school district that attempts to teach African American children a survival of the fittest lifestyle and that they are islands unto themselves.

Creative Learning Techniques

If we are going to educate African American children effectively, we need to change many of the learning techniques used in schools. The buddy system is an excellent way to influence the peer dynamic and acknowledge African values. Classrooms can be divided into pairs and buddies become responsible for each other. It is naïve for us to expect African American children who do everything together at home, in the community, on the playground, and in the park to be individualists in the classroom.

Low achieving and disadvantaged students are almost by definition unable to compete in regular school programs. Competition for them means coming in last and getting failing grades. In cooperative learning programs, all students must perform well. It is the role of each student to assist each of the other students in learning and performing well. No one is to fail. No one is to come in last.

As children help their peers to learn, they continue to grow as well. Chronic failure becomes a thing of the past. Feelings of self-esteem and confidence can reach normal levels. An environment where all students are expected and assisted to do well is a place where a student can feel accepted and secure. Cooperative learning arrangements create mentally healthy environments for students.

Children who fail in competitive grade-oriented classrooms need a cooperative learning approach to keep them from becoming casualties. Competition is only motivating for those students who have the skills to win. Grades are only motivating for those students who can get good ones. In competitive instructional programs, low achieving students, by definition, always finish last. It is demoralizing for them.

In competitive environments where low-achievers realize that there is little hope of doing well, there is a strong temptation to cheat. There is little temptation to cheat when everyone is supposed to do well. Cooperative learning arrangements benefit low-achieving and disadvantaged students. Because students are expected to help and learn from one another, cheating will not be an issue and discipline problems are reduced.

I enjoyed observing one first grade teacher who actually required her students to answer questions simultaneously. This "choral" approach works and meshes with peer dynamics and is true cooperation at its best. Responding together is fun, so students remain alert during class. Their confidence grows as they answer correctly, and they do not suffer the humiliation of answering incorrectly on their own or not answering at all. Their response will be right the next time, given that questions can be repeated several times. The choral response also gives security to the shy child.

Gender Learning Differences

Divide and conquer the peer group by identifying the leader of the classroom and instilling your values into him. Once students see that their leader has bought into academic achievement, self-discipline, etc., they too will get on board. Two strategies are effective in dividing the peer group: the jigsaw method and the team-assisted approach.

Jigsaw Method. Let's say you have 30 students divided into 6 teams of 5 students, each of whom receives a number from 1 to 5. The assignment is to write a report and make a presentation on the life of Martin Luther King, Jr. The one's in each team will have to learn about King's childhood. The two's will learn about his life at Morehouse University. The three's will examine his theories of nonviolence that he learned from Mahatma Gandhi. The four's will study his family. The five's will explore his career.

The beauty of the jigsaw method is that teams are dependent on each other to complete the project and achieve a good grade. In this way you can team an A student with a D student, but the A student will not successfully pass without acquiring information from the D student. The jigsaw method makes everyone dependent on each other and makes everyone important. They realize that they are only as strong as the weakest link.

Team-Assisted Approach. In this approach, the teacher divides the children based on ability so that every team will have an A, B, C, D, and F student. There is an equitable distribution of students in each group, and they learn from each other. One of the benefits of this kind of cooperative learning is that it discourages grading on a curve. In a typical classroom where teachers grade on the curve, the students with the highest grades are resented. Using the team-assisted approach, students help each other do well because if every member of their team scores well, it improves the overall score for the team.

Academic Awards. It is amazing that schools give more accolades to athletic achievement than academic achievement. Every school should have academic assembly programs. Unfortunately, because schools operate from a middleclass, individualistic, competitive value system, awards are given only to the few. Therefore, African American youth who operate from a different value system do not buy into academic achievement, and they still view those few successful students as nerds.

An Nguzo Saba assembly program, in which everyone is eligible for an award, would be a way to acknowledge more students for their efforts. If a student moves from a D to a C, they receive an award. If a student moves from a C to an A, they receive two awards. Possibly every student could receive an award, and we could begin to make academic achievement attractive to Black students.

Teaching to Succeed

It is unfortunate that even in the 21st century, American schools are still highly segregated in terms of activities. A school can be integrated yet still have all Black players on the basketball team and all White members in the science club and debate team. Given Black male appreciation of "the dozens," rap "battling," and general verbal sparring, participating on debate teams would be an excellent activity for such fluent, creative speakers who can think quickly on their feet.

Over the past decade, Jeff Howard, through his Efficacy Committee, has studied the psychology of success. Howard's research has helped me better understand why 200 students are willing to try out for 12 basketball slots but are unwilling to try for slots on the debate team or science fair team, where the percentages are more in their favor. What explains this behavior? Howard discovered that people who feel good about themselves attribute their successes and failures to their abilities

112

and/or effort. This keeps them always in control. If they fail, they know they simply have to increase time on task. They understand that the secret to success is that whatever you do most will be what you do best.

Students who are not confident of their abilities tend to attribute their success or failure to luck or the nature of the task. They attribute failure to lack of ability. Therefore, if they did well on a math test, they would feel it was because of luck or that the test was easy. If they failed the test, they would say they are not good in math so there is no need for further study.

African Americans have bought into the negative psychology of success and have convinced themselves that they are better in sports than science, better in music than math, better in rap than reading. African American students need to take a class in the psychology of performance. They need to understand the related significance of ability, luck, effort, and the nature of the task. They must realize that success should be attributed to ability and effort and failure to lack of endeavor. In this way they are always in control of the situation.

Schools spend so much time discussing irrelevant issues, but this very important concept is not taught to children. As we begin to teach students how to think about success in ways that will empower them, we will begin to channel their abilities, intelligence, and energy.

Channeling Energy

A social worker once said to me, *"The root of the problem in our school district is that we do not know how to channel Black male energy."* I have written about this subject in my books, but I could not have stated the problem more succinctly. We must do a better job of channeling Black male energy. It is criminal that schools have opted to put Black boys in the corner, send them to the principal's office for suspension and expulsion, and place them in special education rather than properly channeling their energy.

Why is it that in most elementary schools physical education is offered once a week and at high schools, it is offered daily? One of the best ways to channel male energy is by offering physical education classes daily at every grade level.

Every school should offer martial arts, not for combat training but to teach African American males self-discipline while releasing some of their energy. In my book *State of Emergency: We Must Save African American Males,* I describe how schools are now being built without playgrounds, and recess has been removed from the daily schedule. While I understand that some schools have eliminated recess for security reasons, this is a critical mistake and short-sighted, especially given the disproportionate percentage of African American males in special education because of ADD and ADHD diagnoses. Every school needs to offer recess and provide playground space and equipment. If we know that boys have a short attention span, when are teachers going to meet this reality by incorporating more physical activity into the lesson plan?

One innovative primary grade teacher infuses her daily phonics lesson with physical exercises. Children do jumping jacks, push-ups, sit-ups, and run in place as they recite the letters of the alphabet and their phonemic sounds. There is a lot of noise and movement in this group, but children love it. Teachers can also apply this idea to multiplication tables, names of states—any list that students must memorize. Parents love this activity too because children sleep soundly during the night and concepts are instilled in a non-boring, painless, fun way. Also, upon the conclusion of every lesson, teachers should allow a five-minute break for students to stretch, perform push-ups, or do something physical before moving on to the next mental exercise.

As I discuss in my book *Satan, I'm Taking Back My Health,* from the early 1900s to the present, we have increased

Gender Learning Differences

our average sugar consumption from 4 pounds annually to 155 pounds. Our bodies were not designed to absorb that much sugar; therefore our children go through sugar irregularities throughout the day. One of the most effective ways to redirect children's energy is to reduce their sugar consumption. Schools have the power to eliminate sugar from the school diet. I am heartened to hear that a movement is emerging in some enlightened schools to remove soda and junk food from vending machines and replace them with healthier juices and snacks (e.g., fruit). This is a good first step, but more needs to be done.

To close this chapter on gender learning differences, I would like to discuss the almost two-to-one ratio of African American females to males in college. What's even more difficult to explain is the almost 20 percent difference in the graduation rates of African American females to males. This disparity even takes place at Black colleges, so African American males cannot use the race card to explain why she graduated from Howard University and he did not.

There are numerous reasons for this phenomenon. Some mothers raise their daughters and love their sons, as the saying goes. Girls have many role models at home and in the classroom, but boys do not. Many boys have gone from kindergarten through eighth grade without a male teacher. The following quote best describes this phenomenon:

> Girls come to school to learn. Boys have to be driven. Many girls will work at a subject they dislike. No healthy boy ever does. In a study on Black boys, Mary Fuller talks about how girls develop a pro-education and anti-school position. They adopt a pragmatic approach to schooling: it is a means to an end. They can do this without investing much value in White teachers and a White curriculum. The cost of directly attacking schools was too high for them. This was a strategy of resistance within accommodation.[50]

Let's recap the major gender differences and how schools should adjust.

Gender Differences

Male Characteristic	School Adjustment
Shorter attention span	Shorten the lesson plan and/or gear lessons toward male interests.
Less developed in fine motor skills	Lower penmanship, handwriting writing and cursive expectations.
Greater energy level	Allow more movement and exercise through the day.
Less hearing ability	Speak louder, have boys sit closer to the front, and understand why boys are louder.
Slower maturation	Allow for the differences, especially in reading, and either avoid comparing boys to girls or create single-gender groups within the class.
Not as neat	Alter expectations, assist them and provide more organizing time and tools.
Less cooperative	Understand that most boys are not teacher pleasers and desire greater male influence. Consider inviting male role models to speak to your class.
Influenced more by peer group	Never embarrass him in front of his peer group. Consider implementing cooperative learning and peer tutoring.
More aggressive	Understand the showdown, the dozens, and the need for boys to resolve conflict. Provide nonviolent, physical opportunities to achieve this, e.g., Native American hand wrestling.

Gender Learning Differences

I hope this chapter on gender differences has been helpful. We can reduce the number of African American males in special education if we understand, appreciate, and allow for gender differences. Historically it has not been the teacher's fault. Unfortunately, most teachers in their training years were never given a course in male learning styles, specifically African American male learning styles.

I cannot emphasize enough that this problem is not just germane to African American male students. In America, White males are placed in special education 200 percent more frequently than White females. This is not a *race* issue. This is a *gender* issue. My prayer is that as White female teachers make the necessary adjustments for their male students and sons, those benefits will spill over to African American boys as well.

In the next chapter, we will look at the most important meeting of the Black boy's life: the IEP (Individualized Educational Plan).

CHAPTER 8: THE IEP

Dear Parent:

I am very concerned about ____'s ability to function in school, both in the large classroom and in the small group setting. It has been my observation over the past month that ____ is unable to maintain attention or remain seated for more than a few minutes. His excessive movement and impulsivity (e.g., talking out inappropriately in class, frequently falling from his chair, doing flips in class) are extremely disruptive and have a strong negative impact on his ability to achieve.

____ is also more than a year behind in reading and is missing much teacher instruction because he is unable to settle down, listen, follow directions, and follow-through on assignments. I believe ____ wants to comply with rules and behavioral expectations to please me, however, a great many of his behaviors seem to be beyond his control and awareness. I have already moved ____ several times because he is unable to sit near the other children without bothering them constantly.

He is unable to complete any assignment without someone sitting directly with him, keeping him on task, and focused.

We are going to try to have ____ use a study carrel (partitioned space) to help block out distractions and give him more space. We are also going to begin a behavioral contract to use in the classroom for monitoring ____'s behavior, and we will be communicating with you on a daily basis.

____ is a very likable and affectionate boy. We are all willing and eager to do whatever is necessary and possible to help him succeed at our school.

However, he is probably in need of more assistance than we are able to provide for him. We have a number of students at this school with medically diagnosed ADD/ADHD. We request your attendance at an IEP (Individualized Education Plan) meeting to determine the next step.

Sincerely,
Classroom Teacher

The dreaded letter has arrived. This is every parent's nightmare. Parents love their children dearly and pray that they will have a successful school career. Unfortunately, this is not the case for large numbers of African American children and specifically, African American males.

The Individualized Educational Plan (IEP) is the most important meeting of the Black boy's life. This meeting will determine whether he will stay in the regular classroom or whether he will receive special education services. If he is to receive special education services, will they be included in the regular classroom, will he spend time in a resource room, or will he go to a separate classroom or residential facility?

The meeting is scheduled on a weekday at 12:00, but, strangely, five or six professionals arrive at 11:30. The team includes the regular classroom teacher, a special education teacher or coordinator, a psychologist, social worker or counselor, sometimes a physician, and the principal. I wonder why they arrived earlier. I wonder what they discussed. There have been horror stories of plans that were already written before the official meeting with the parent took place. This is in clear violation of IDEA legislation.

Why is the meeting scheduled for the convenience of the team when professionals are always so critical about the lack of parental involvement? IEPs, PTA meetings, graduations, and assemblies are scheduled for the benefit of educators, not parents. Can you imagine if Wal-Mart decided that they would

The IEP

only open between 9:00 and 3:00, Monday through Friday? They would lose money. Could the reason for this schedule be because so many educators no longer live in the communities where they teach and have no intention or desire to return during the evening? If we really want to make this meeting fair for parents, we should schedule the meeting at a time that is more beneficial for them.

The low-income single female parent arrives at 12:00. Can you imagine how she must feel when she enters the room and the professional team is sitting around the table with their papers? She knows she has been talked about. She knows that the decision has been made, her child has already been placed, and her appearance is purely a formality. People who are self-centered cannot imagine how stressful this is because people with power do not place themselves in situations where they do not have the upper hand.

This meeting is even more intimidating if the four or five professionals are all White, which is probably the case. The only African American present is usually the parent. The parent is outnumbered. In most cases, the parent does not have the professional and educational expertise of the team. She or he is at a clear disadvantage.

If O.J. Simpson had been tried in Simi Valley or if the police who beat Rodney King had been tried in Los Angeles, the outcomes would have been different. Parents need a Johnnie Cochran or Willie Gary to have the venue of the meeting changed and to ensure that the IEP team reflects the racial make-up of the child.

In my book *Black Students—Middle-Class Teachers*, I mention that the middleclass mentality of team professionals is also a significant issue in the IEP process. Having African Americans on the team does not guarantee that they will have the best interests of Black boys in mind. Like Supreme Court

Justice Clarence Thomas, they may not make decisions from an African American-centered viewpoint. Sometimes a progressive White member of the team may be more supportive of the African American parent and child than an African American professional.

Let's describe the flow of the IEP process and the starting line-up of the professional team.

1. The regular classroom teacher has decided that the African American male needs to be removed from her classroom. There is a good chance that she has never taken a class in Black history, Black culture, Black learning styles, or Black male learning styles and has not read any books on this subject. Earlier we mentioned that 20 percent of the teachers make 80 percent of the referrals. She is also aware that her recommendation carries the most weight in this meeting and that 92 percent of the children referred to special education are tested and 73 percent of them are placed. She also feels that because she is exposed to the child more than any other professional, she is in the best position to make the recommendation for special education placement.

2. The psychologist has a long list of tests to choose from. Unfortunately, most psychologists would not consider the Black Intelligence Test of Cultural Homogeneity, the System of Multicultural Pluralistic Assessment (SOMPA), the Learning Potential Assessment Device (LPAD), the Cognitive Assessment System (CAS), or the Kaufman Test of Educational Achievement. The two most popular tests that the psychologist will consider will be the Weschler Intelligence Scale for Children and the Stanford Binet Intelligence Scale.

3. The physician or psychiatrist will make a recommendation without ever giving the child a physical exam.

The IEP

4. The special education coordinator, social worker, counselor, and principal are primarily present in a perfunctory role. They are overwhelmed with the tremendous amount of work they have and meetings to attend. They are present only because they are required. Social workers and counselors have huge caseloads and are often responsible for several schools. The principal, who not only is the CEO for the building but also the instructional leader, has probably more than 100 agenda items that must be covered this day. This IEP meeting is just one item on the agenda.

IDEA requires that the following six components be included in the IEP:

1. A statement of the child's present level of educational performance (academics, behavior issues, strengths, and needs).
2. A statement of annual goals and short-term instructional objectives, plus expected achievement for each area in which the student is experiencing difficulties.
3. A statement of specific educational services to be provided for the child and the extent to which the child will participate in regular educational programs. Includes special education programs, accommodations, and related services.
4. The projected dates for initiation of services and the anticipated duration.
5. Appropriate objective criteria and evaluation procedures and schedules for determining whether the short-term instructional objectives are being achieved.
6. Individualized transition planning by age 14 or earlier.

In the excellent book *Writing Measurable IEP Goals and Objectives,* Barbara Bateman provides the following about IEPs:

> Sadly, many professionals who work with Individualized Educational Plans, if given the chance, would vote to abolish them. IEPs have taken up several hundred million hours of special education personnel time (a conservative estimate) that most teachers would far rather have spent in direct teaching with students. This has to change. Society cannot, nor should it continue to invest this much time and money with little benefit to show for it.[52]

Two aspects of the IEP deserve special notice. First, the IEP is an individualized program, which means that the IEP should include information about the needs of a specific child, not the teacher or administration. But what exactly does the child need? The third component of the IEP attempts to answer this question: "A statement of specific educational services to be provided for the child." The operative word is "specific."

Special education is not a place but a service. Yet many IEPs are filled with information explaining whether the service is going to take place in the regular classroom, the resource room, or a separate classroom. Often they do not address what type of educational service is to be rendered.

In a scathing document titled "The Road to Nowhere: The Illusion and Broken Promises of Special Education in Baltimore City and Other Public School Systems," Attorney Kalman Hettleman states:

> In one common scenario a child classified as LD is in the fourth grade. The IEP team first determines measurable goals and objectives, that is, how much progress the child is supposed to achieve over the next year. Then the IEP team determines whether the teaching is to take place inside or outside the general education classroom

The IEP

(least restrictive environment) and sets the number of hours of special education instruction and other services. However, IEP teams almost never discuss or prescribe, for example, the instructional content and methods, pupil-teacher ratio, and teacher training. IEPs for students are virtually silent on these basic design questions, despite the training mantra that special education is a service, not a place.

In fact, IEP teams do just the opposite. They focus foremost on the legal mandate that students receive their special education services in the least restrictive environment (LRE). LRE usually means an inclusion placement in general education classrooms with predominantly nondisabled students for most of the school day rather than separation in a pullout group, a self-contained classroom, or a school with only disabled students. But the LRE placement determines only where the services will be rendered, not what essential elements of instruction will be.

Two prominent inclusion experts have summarized the research: regardless of classroom placement, the necessity remains to develop and implement effective instructional methods to increase the opportunities that these students have for learning important academic material, as well as for increasing the rate to which these skills are developed. At IEP meetings, Baltimore Public Schools defends the absence of specific instructional plans incorporating the research-based practices on the grounds that IEPs are not supposed to prescribe methods of instruction. As special educators put it, IEPs are supposed to state what goals and objectives are to be achieved, but not how to achieve them.

As a result, the how, the specific instruction or design, is left up to the student's teachers, who are not trained in research-based instructional programs and practices. By this refusal to prescribe methods of instruction when appropriate, the IEPs violate federal and state regulations. IDEA regulations state that specially designed instruction means adapting as appropriate the content, methodology, or delivery of instruction.[53]

Barbara Bateman reinforces Hettleman's observations:

What is a parent to understand about the actual services being delivered to the child when all the IEP says is two hours of special education daily? Does that mean one-to-one, small group, resource room with 20 students present, a combination or none of the above? Is it with an aide, a regular education teacher, a special education teacher, an emergency certified teacher, or other? Is it discovery-based learning, direct instruction, cooperative learning, or other?[54]

If we acknowledge that 80 percent of the special education students referred are below grade level in reading, the IEP should document something different from what is already being provided in the regular classroom. We must first acknowledge failure in the regular education classroom. Not the failure of the student, but the failure of the regular education classroom to teach the boy how to read. Consequently, an IEP is inadequate and incomplete if it does not address the major issue that occurs 80 percent of the time, which is the inability of Black boys to read at grade level. Therefore, we are not as concerned about where the new instruction is going to take place as we are about what the instruction will entail. Continuing to do what we have been doing and expecting a different outcome is insanity. The IEP should have a different curriculum, a different pedagogy in order to initiate real change.

The IEP

As we discussed earlier, one of the major reasons for poor reading scores is too little emphasis on phonics instruction. Therefore, the IEP should include, when needed, i.e., 80 percent of the time, phonics instruction. But it is not enough to simply say phonics instruction. The IEP should identify which curriculum will be used to teach phonics. Open Court, Orton-Gillingham, Hooked On Phonics, Go Phonics, and Modern Curriculum Press are all excellent programs.

Psychologists should assess children's learning styles. If a child is found to be a right-brain learner, then the IEP should include mostly right-brain lesson plans, with the emphases being visual, kinesthetic, and tactile. Where these lessons will take place is not as significant as the determination that there will be a change in the pedagogy from left-brain to right-brain.

The team must address the fact that Black children do not see themselves in the curriculum. There is a direct correlation between attention span and interest. If we capture students' interest, the attention span will increase. If we provide them with an irrelevant curriculum, the attention span will decrease. Schools must make their curricula more multicultural and Africentric. We recommend the excellent curriculum SETCLAE (Self-Esteem Through Culture Leads to Academic Excellence). This curriculum has ready-made lesson plans, textbooks, and supplementary books to enhance self-esteem and reinforce language arts and social study skills.

If we understand that many of the boys who are being recommended for special education have a high energy level and are aggressive, then daily physical education (PE) must be included in any IEP. Elementary school children need PE just as much as teens in high school. Even if there is no recess or playground, the classroom teacher can still incorporate exercise and movement into the lesson plan.

When appropriate, include cooperative learning and peer tutoring opportunities into the IEP. Utilize the power of the peer group to reinforce the value of academic achievement.

Single-gender classrooms may be an effective alternative to special education. If, as a principal, you find that many boys in your school are being placed in special education, consider creating single-gender classrooms instead. As long as boys and girls have equal access to resources and information, you have complied with Title 9 legislation. Boys are not deficient but simply different from girls. Boys and girls can both benefit from this arrangement as it reduces distractions.

The professional IEP team reminds me of Code Blue in the police department, where loyalty to fellow officers is more important than loyalty to the people they are supposed to protect and serve. In the excellent book *Racial Inequity in Special Education,* edited by Gary Orfield, the following questions raise the issue of a Code Blue mentality that taints the entire IEP process:

1. What roles do teachers play in formal diagnosis and assessment?
2. What role do the preconceptions of school personnel about the child's family circumstances play in the assessment?
3. To what extent is the assessment affected by external pressures for identification and placement?
4. What role does the classroom ecology play in the learning or behavioral difficulties exhibited by the child?
5. How is the assessment affected by the way disability categories are defined and operationalized?
6. What factors influence psychologists' selections of instruments to conduct the assessment?

Let's review the IEP process thus far.

The central role of the referring teaching has been documented by a long line of research. Gerber and Semmel argue that teachers' perceptions of the reasons for children's learning difficulties were a very good predictor of what would be found by the psychological assessment, and the teachers' judgments could be as reliable as those of the psychologists. Other researchers have corroborated this idea, e.g., Gresham, Reschly, Carey, Shinn, Tindal, and Spira. It is certainly well known that 80 percent or greater of referred students will be identified as having a disability, and several scholars have pointed to the teacher's decision to refer as the key to the entire process.

In another school a teacher expressed dismay after a team conference because he felt the psychologist had expected him to agree with her recommendation that a child be placed on medication for hyperactivity. The teacher felt that the psychologist had been pushing her own agenda and had not validated his effort to work with the child in the classroom. Our data also indicate examples where the teacher's diagnosis is not corroborated by the psychological evaluation. However, in these cases the psychologist may have social consequences to meet as a result of his or her determination.

For example, one psychologist found that a child referred for emotional disturbance did not qualify for service under that disability. The school staff involved were irate when they heard that this was the outcome of the assessment, and they went to the conference ready to do battle with the psychologist. However, this psychologist solved the "problem" by classifying the child as eligible for services under ADHD. Another psychologist, quite open about the pressure from administrators and teachers, had indicated that she does her best to meet these needs by choosing instruments that will be likely to "find" the disability suspected by school personnel.

> When a student is found to qualify for a special education service based on the psychologist's assessment, this is considered a validation for the referring teacher. The school district keeps track of how many students are referred and placed in each school, and those teachers and schools that have a high percentage of referred students qualifying are praised since their referrals are seen as having been appropriate.[55]

This is absolutely ludicrous. We are talking about children. We are talking about people's lives. I believe there is a relationship between Ritalin and cocaine, between special education and prison, between illiteracy and incarceration. For some school districts to literally define success based on the relationship between referrals and placement illustrates how acute and severe is the problem.

My prayer is that the latest IDEA legislation passed by Congress will have the teeth to circumvent schools that boast of their IEP team's placement of children. In addition, success should not be based on the number of children who stay in regular classrooms and must endure the same ineffective, irrelevant pedagogy and curricula.

Finally, I want to ask every IEP team member across America, Can you in good conscience answer to God that you made the best and most objective decision you could?

Evaluating the IEP

1. Reveals how to measure whether the goal has been accomplished.
2. Yields the same conclusion if measured by several people.
3. Allows the calculation of how much progress it represents.
4. Can be measured without additional information.

Evaluation is often seen as a dry statistical exercise, but if designed, implemented, and interpreted well, this important activity can shed a lot of light on how well, or poorly, the IEP and special education are serving Black schoolboys. Evaluating IEPs and special education programs should enlighten teachers and administrators and stimulate real change in the system. Evaluation results should be used as a tool to constantly refine and update both the IEP and the entire program.

Historically, evaluation has been as relevant as the IEP goals and objectives that it measures. Isn't it interesting that evaluation of special education programs seldom look at whether a boy is returned to the mainstream classroom in a specific amount of time? That's because this goal usually is not addressed in the IEP meeting and thus does not come up during evaluation.

If we begin to ask better questions during evaluation, we should begin to see a dramatic reduction in the number of Black boys being placed in special education programs. As our goals and objectives for keeping Black boys out of special education change, we will begin to ask brand new questions of our programs. We will begin to place demands on the system to better serve the learning needs of Black boys.

To evaluate a special education program in this new light, let us ask:

1. What percentage of special education students return to the mainstream classroom and at what grade level?
2. What percentage of special education students show reduced behavioral problems?
3. What percentage of special education students graduate from high school?
4. What makes special education "special?" What is done in the special education class that is different from the regular class?
5. Does special education offer higher expectations?
6. Does special education make the curriculum more relevant?
7. Does special education use more right-brain lesson plans?

Not only do IEPs not provide details of the services to be rendered but the goals are so nebulous, esoteric, and vague that they cannot be measured. An IEP goal might be something as vague as "appreciating art," "enjoying literature," "understanding history," "becoming independent," "respecting authority," "increasing listening skills," "increasing basic and other life skills," and "becoming successful in the mainstream class." I have described many of the problems inherent in the IEP process. The following describes the characteristics of a successful IEP.

1. A successful IEP meeting provides respect to all of its members.
2. The members of the professional team come to the meeting with an open mind.
3. Parents are made to feel comfortable.
4. Ideally, as in a doctoral oral exam, the parents should lead the committee to further enhance the parents' comfort level.
5. The regular classroom teacher's power should be minimized. We can no longer accept 20 percent of the teachers making 80 percent of the referrals and almost 90 percent of children recommended for special education being placed. That is too great a concentration of power.
6. We must eliminate the colleague loyalty conspiracy among IEP team members.
7. The IEP must clearly describe what type of curriculum and pedagogy is going to be provided.
8. There should be clearly stated, measurable goals: "Willie is placed in special education for one year. He presently is two years behind in reading. We are going to provide Open Court Phonics, SETCLAE, and single-gender classrooms. The objective is to return Willie to the mainstream classroom at grade level, without any test accommodations and without social promotion, within one year."
9. IEPs do not need to be a 50- to 100-page document that fails to get to the root of the problem. Barbara Bateman says that the quality of an IEP is not based on the number

The IEP

of pages but its content. Therefore, a successful IEP can be less than 10 pages long.

Parental Rights

There is a 68 percent chance that the parent will be female and a one-in-three chance that she will be living under the poverty level and possess only a high school education. In addition, there is a good chance that she will not be represented by a lawyer, minister, or community advocate, although it is her right. Parents must know their rights before going into this all-important meeting. Do your homework. Your child's very future is at stake.

1. Your child cannot be tested without your consent, but once you give your consent, the outcome of the test can be used to place your child in special education.
2. You have every right to recommend that the test reflect your family's culture. Fight against the use of the Weschler and Stanford-Binet, and advocate for any or all of the following tests (ranked in order of cultural significance): Black Intelligence Test of Cultural Homogeneity, the System of Multicultural Pluralistic Assessment (SOMPA), the Learning Potential Assessment Device (LPAD), the Cognitive Assessment System (CAS), the Kaufman Test of Educational Achievement.
3. The school cannot place your child in special education without your permission. They can disagree with your decision, which will result in three options being available: (a) you can request a hearing; (b) you can suggest mediation; (c) you can request an Independent Education Evaluation, which would involve non-school personnel.
4. The school cannot give your children medications without your permission. Before accepting a prescription for Ritalin, insist that a medical exam be conducted. Even then, proceed with caution. Ritalin is a dangerous drug.

5. Do not feel rushed in the IEP meeting. Do not make any decision or sign any document unless you are absolutely sure that this is the right approach to take for your son or daughter. In fact, wait 24 hours before making a decision. Take the IEP document to someone you trust for review. Ideally, that person should attend the meeting with you—someone with a degree, someone with experience in education if possible. Do not attend the meeting by yourself. Also, ask the principal for a list of parents who have attended IEPs over the past 12 months so you can network with them and strategize.
6. You have a right to review all records in your child's file. Read everything in your child's file. This will help you assess whether the referral was a teacher's knee-jerk reaction or if there really is a problem.
7. Ask the principal which teachers in the school make the most referrals into special education. Make sure your child is not placed in those classrooms.
8. In reviewing the IEP, remember the special education mantra that it is not a place but a service. The IEP should clearly spell out two major concerns: (a) what pedagogy and curriculum will be used to help the child; (b) what will be the measurable outcome of this change?

Parents, ultimately your child's life is in your hands, and there is a lot you can do to turn things around for your son. Regardless of how the school made you feel, you were not powerless in this situation. In fact, you are the final authority when it comes to all matters regarding your children. Parents, I suggest if your child's teacher is considering special education, you give the teacher this book and politely ask them to read it before making a final decision.

In the next chapter, we will look at the role parents can play in reducing the number of African American males in special education. Parents also can do a lot more at home to effectively complement classroom work.

CHAPTER 9: PARENT EMPOWERMENT

Empowered parents feel the school works for them, while disempowered parents feel threatened by the school. I wish parents could hear what some teachers say about their children in the teachers' lounge. Schools should open the teachers' lounge to parents—not that I think teachers would make derogatory comments in their presence, but it would serve as a deterrent.

Suppose Mrs. Little, Malcolm X's mother, heard one teacher tell another that her son could never be a lawyer and should consider becoming a carpenter. All parents should visit their child's school and, if at all possible, visit the teachers' lounge either before school or during lunchtime.

Parents tell me that they cringe whenever they receive a call from the school. Unfortunately, most schools only interact with parents when there is bad news. Earlier, I mentioned that many teachers only give attention to students when they are negative. In St. Louis, I met a teacher who had a "negative" section of the room for all students who behaved inappropriately. When I asked her if she had a positive section of the room, she said no.

Parents tell me they only hear from schools when there is negative news. Wouldn't it be nice if schools flipped the script and called parents with good news? How refreshing it would be for a parent to be called because the child received an A or B on a quiz or showed leadership in the classroom.

There is a class conflict between African American students and middleclass schools. This chapter will attempt to describe some of the class conflicts that exist between schools and African American parents. The following are some examples of how schools are middleclass institutions and the challenges this presents for many African American parents.

During the school day the teacher reviewed math problems 1–10 and assigned for homework problems 11–20. But there was one additional step in problems 11–20 that had not been discussed during the school day. The teacher expected the parent to become the assistant teacher and tutor the child on materials that were not covered in school. This is acceptable if the parents have the educational background to provide this service. For many middleclass students, that becomes the norm. Could it be that many middleclass teachers assume their students come from middleclass families and that the parents are as knowledgeable as they are?

This may explain why many African American children's scores decline from the fourth grade on: as the difficulty of homework assignments increases, students receive less support at home. Many teachers expect that a middleclass, educated parent is at home and will serve as assistant teacher when this might not be the case.

As we discussed earlier, scheduling the IEP meeting at 12:00 is a problem. Suppose the parent(s) has to work? Again, we see that schools design the process to meet their own needs, not those of parents.

Throughout this book I have been critical of schools and what I feel are their shortcomings. But schools only have children from 9:00 am to 3:00 pm, Monday through Friday, for about 180 days per year. Parents have children from 3:00 until the next morning, all weekend, holidays, and summers for a minimum of 18 years. Clearly, in a child's development the greater influence is exerted by the parents.

There is a science to being a parent, and where in America do we learn the necessary skills? For many of us, parenting has been trial and error, or we raise children the way we were raised. Maybe we have raised one child in one manner and another child in another. I invite parents to take the following test. In areas of parenting, grade yourself from A to F. Have your children grade you, too. Take the following quiz and let's see how well you do.

Parent Empowerment

	A	B	C	D	F
1. Have you helped your children develop goals?					
2. Are your children self-disciplined?					
3. Are you consistent?					
4. Do you give your children quality time?					
5. Do you show affection?					
6. How well do you monitor peer pressure?					
7. Do you monitor television viewing?					
8. Do you listen to their music?					
9. Do you provide your children with a nutritional diet?					
10. Do your children receive an adequate amount of sleep?					
11. Do you express high expectations for your children?					
12. Are you a positive role model?					
13. How well do you listen?					
14. How frequently do you visit the school?					
15. Do you take your children on field trips?					
16. Could your children construct a family tree?					
17. Do your children understand the value of prayer?					

It is possible to average an A on this test notwithstanding that your children still have problems in school. God has given our children free will. Regardless of what we do as parents, the final decision for their behavior rests with them.

Yet it is safe to say that children are affected by the quality of parenting. We can reduce the odds of our children being placed in special education, suspended, expelled, and doing poorly academically if we work on developing better parenting skills in ways suggested by the above questions.

Just as I can determine the values of a teacher by observing his or her classroom, the décor, bulletin boards, lesson plans, and library books, so can I determine the values of parents. The way parents decorate and fill their homes tells a lot about the type of child that comes out of the house. Engineers, doctors, and lawyers need certain things in their homes in order to develop. Ball players and rappers need certain things in their homes in order to develop.

If I visited your house, what would I see? Would I see more CDs, videos, and DVDs than books? Would I see a television with cable in every room? Would I find a computer with Internet access? What do you have in your home? The following is a list of items that I believe every African American household must have and display prominently. If you do not have these items, I encourage you to secure them immediately.

- Bible
- Atlas
- Globe
- Dictionary
- Thesaurus
- Encyclopedia
- Computer
- Internet access
- Microscope

Parent Empowerment

- Chemistry set
- Telescope
- Educational games
- Library card
- Dominoes
- Chess
- Checkers
- Scrabble

As an educational consultant, not only do I spend time working with teachers and students but many principals will also have me speak to their PTA. Many principals tell me that they do not expect a significant number of parents to attend. It is embarrassing to have a school with 300 families and only 10 parents attend a meeting.

Over the years, I have observed that some schools have more success at attracting parents then others. Listed below are some of the techniques these schools use to increase parent attendance at PTA meetings:

1. Make parents feel important.
2. Provide a parent room.
3. Provide tutorial, computer, and job-training sessions in the school.
4. Hire a parent coordinator.
5. Sensitize clerical staff to welcome parents.
6. Encourage parents to visit the classrooms.
7. Let parents choose the PTA topics.
8. Let parents choose the day, time, and location of PTA meetings, which will often be at a church or community organization rather than at the school.
9. Invite a dynamic speaker.
10. Provide transportation.
11. Provide childcare.
12. Offer a door prize.

13. Offer a prize for the classroom with the largest parent attendance.
14. Provide food—not just refreshments but a full meal.
15. Have children perform.

When schools implement the above, they succeed in increasing parent involvement. Notice I did not suggest that schools pay parents to attend the meeting. I have a major problem and disdain for schools that feel the only way to attract parents is to pay them.

As it relates to special education, I have a greater problem with parents who would sell their children down the river for what has often been called the "crazy check." Several years ago, social security was expanded to include not only children with significant limitations in life functioning but also those with limitations that are more moderate. SSI was expanded to include children with lesser disabilities. Those deemed eligible received back payments with interest.

During 2004 regulations were tightened because some parents were abusing the system to secure "crazy checks." Can you imagine a parent actually placing their child in special education in order to receive an additional $400 per month? Poverty will make you do foolish things, but there is nothing so foolish as to sell your child into special education when only 6 percent return to the mainstream classroom on grade level, only 27 percent graduate, and 40 percent become addicted to illegal drugs.

As for the high illiteracy rates in this country, parents can do much to help their children learn to read. Earlier, I asked whether we have a special education problem or a reading problem. The answer, in large degree, is that we have a reading problem, and parents can be part of the solution. If we teach our children how to read, we can reduce the disproportionate number of African American males placed in special education. Is there anything parents could do better in preparing their children for reading?

Parent Empowerment

There is a wide disparity in American homes in the area of literacy. We cannot blame schools for this. Some children enter kindergarten with more than 20,000 hours of exposure to books. Their parents have read to them, some even when their children were still in the womb. There are other children who have spent less than 10 hours with a book in their hands upon entering kindergarten. Some haven't even seen a book or opened the pages of one. They do not appreciate or know what a book is. We cannot blame the classroom teacher for this disparity, can we?

Some parents not only listen to their children but they speak to them. They speak in complete sentences. They do not talk "baby talk" to them. They help nurture their vocabulary. As a result, some children by the age of five have been exposed to 45 million words. Unfortunately, there are other children who have been exposed to less than 4 million words, most of which were heard on television and rap videos.

Reading is one of Bill Cosby's major concerns. We as parents must make our children the priority. Something is drastically wrong when parents tell the principal that they do not have a dollar for a field trip while smoking a cigarette in the principal's face. Cosby was on point when he suggested that some parents would buy their children a $200 pair of sneakers but would not purchase Hooked On Phonics for their youngsters. It has been said that some parents buy what they want and beg for what they need.

Listed below are the major influences ranked in order of their importance to our children.

1950	Present
home	peer pressure
school	rap music
church	television
peer	home
television	school

If you want to be an effective parent in this new millennium, you must know your children's friends. You must listen to their music, and you must monitor what your children watch on television. Unfortunately in many homes presently church is no longer a top priority. A family that prays together stays together. There is power in the Word. The greatest gift you can give to your children is a personal relationship with a Savior who said, "I will never leave you or forsake you."

Ask yourself the following questions and answer as honestly as possible.

Peer Pressure

1. Do you know your children's friends?
2. Do you invite them over to know them better?
3. Do you know your children's friend's parents?
4. Do your children know the distinction between a friend and an acquaintance?
5. Do your children think that being smart is acting White?
6. Is your child's peer group promoting and encouraging academic achievement?

Rap Music

1. Do you listen to your children's music?
2. Have you taught your children the distinction between gangster rap and positive rap?
3. Are your children aware that their brains store the lyrics as well as the beat?
4. Do you watch the rap videos with your children and point out that African American females are usually darker than African American males?
5. Do you point out that African American females usually wear less clothing than African American males?

Parent Empowerment

Television

No child watches more television than an African American child does. The average African American child watches almost 40 hours of television per week. That is equivalent to a full-time job. The worst thing one can do for a hyperactive child is to put him or her in front of the television set. Children have become scanners rather than readers as a result of television, with the images changing every second.

> Children who watch more than 10 hours of television a week show lower school achievement. A study by Williams of children in one town before and two years after the introduction of television to their town found that the children showed a decline in reading fluency and creative thinking and increases in verbal and physical aggression. It is estimated that by the age of 18, the average child has witnessed 18,000 murders and over 100,000 violent episodes on television. The National Center for Educational Statistics reports that when parents restrict television viewing, expect their children to make good grades in school, and talk with the child about future educational plans, the children are more likely to stay in school and perform well.[56]

Sonya Carson, the mother of my friend Ben Carson, knew her son was brilliant, but he was failing in school. What did she do? She turned off the television during the week and made Ben and his brother read books and write reports. Just that one change moved Ben Carson from a failing student to someone who is considered one of the best neurosurgeons in the country. Sonya Carson gives the lie to all those who say socioeconomic deprivations cause poor academic performance. She was a single parent. She had a third-grade education and was living below the poverty line. But that did not affect her ability to restrict her children's television viewing.

Another major challenge for parents who are attempting to keep their children out of special education lies in the area of homework. Parents need to do the following:

1. Ask your children if they have homework.
2. Make sure they do their homework as soon as they come home.
3. Homework should be done in a quiet, well-lighted room.
4. If at all possible, check the homework. If unable, ask others (e.g., relatives, church members, school personnel, tutors) who know the subject matter to help.

Many children have homework problems for the following reasons:

1. Does not write down assignment.
2. Writes down the wrong assignment.
3. Forgets the assignment book.
4. Forgets materials needed.
5. Takes hours to do minutes of homework.
6. Hassles about when and where to do homework.
7. Lies about having done homework.
8. Fails to bring notes home concerning homework.
9. Needs constant supervision with homework.
10. Needs constant help with homework.
11. Forgets to get homework papers signed.
12. Forgets and leaves homework at home.

Parents, it is imperative that you assess how your children's school performance may be related to these 12 homework challenges. Do not let your child be placed in special education because he did not do his homework. This is within your power.

Parent Empowerment

Boys often do their homework, but because of their lack of organizational skills, they may forget where they put it. Sometimes it will be in their book bag, but they cannot find it when they get to class. Help your child become more organized. Help him develop a system that he can work with every day. For example, buy a bright, neon-colored homework folder that is only for homework assignments. Make sure that after he completes his homework, the papers go into this folder—not into another folder, folded up and put in his pants pocket, or left lying on the table—this folder and this folder alone. You will have to work with him, but give him time. He will get it eventually, and this will help him to become more organized overall.

In fact, look around his room. Are his clothes in a pile on the floor? Are socks hanging out of drawers? Are toys here and there? Is the bed made up? I know that you just want to close the door so you do not have to look at the mess, but that will not help your son become more organized. Help him create stations for everything, and this will help develop organizational skills. If you help him, he will be thankful in the long run. Sometimes, clean up with him, and do not fuss. As you both are picking things up and putting things away, make jokes, ask him about his day, listen to rap music together, be pleasant. Get into his world, and he will respond positively.

Having read all this, now ask yourself, Could you do better as a parent? What can you do to improve? What can you do better? Is your child underperforming in school because of something in your parenting program? I have been critical of educators and their role in this problem, but parents must also take their share of the responsibility.

As I mentioned, many schools attempt to break the spirits of our boys. As parents, we must do everything we possibly can to prevent this spiritual murder. We must prevent our boys from being shut down, handcuffed, locked up, and taken around in patrol cars.

We must identify our children's interests. God has given all of our children talent, and it is your job as a parent to do whatever you can to find your children's interests. Our children may have a short attention span in one area but a tremendously long attention span in others, as we have seen when they play video games.

Listed below are some of the activities your son may be interested in:

- Airplanes
- Aquariums
- Boats
- Carpentry
- Cars
- Chemistry
- Coin collecting
- Computers
- Drawing
- Electronics
- Geography
- Machines
- Martial arts
- Math
- Microscopes
- Musical instruments
- Pets
- Photography
- Science fiction
- Writing

Mother Love

Mothers, honestly ask yourself if you have double standards for your son and daughter:

Parent Empowerment

1. Do I raise my daughter and love my son?
2. Do I make my daughter come home early but not my son?
3. Do I make my daughter do chores but not my son?
4. Do I make my daughter study more than my son?
5. Do I make my daughter go to church but not my son?
6. Do I expect my daughter to abstain from sex before marriage but not my son?

What are the implications of these double standards? Earlier, we looked at the disproportionate percentage of African American females who graduate from college in comparison to their male counterparts. Do you think that phenomenon only appears at the collegiate level? The following are other ways in which the double standard manifests itself in the African American boy's behaviors and attitudes and in the African American community:

1. Some boys expect the teacher, counselor, psychologist, social worker, principal, coach, employee, police officer, and judge to treat them like their mothers treat them.
2. After hearing it all their lives, some boys begin to believe that they are the man of the house. As a result, a boy will treat his mother like a girlfriend. Is it possible for a nine-year-old boy to be a man? Is it possible to be a man when you have never been in day-to-day contact with one?
3. Some boys will only do chores after a lot of nagging and fussing.
4. There are a large number of mama's boys in the African American community, and this overdependence manifests itself in later years.
5. Many grown African American men are still living at home with their mothers.

6. African American daughters tend to be more responsible than sons.
7. Black women, who are experts on Black men and their behaviors, continue to raise their sons to be near carbon copies of the men they disdain.
8. Teachers and administrators say they want to help children, but mothers may not cooperate and can be hostile and belligerent. Black mothers can be fiercely defensive of their male children. While this is normal mother behavior, it can blind a parent to any real problems that could be going on with their son. Is this phenomenon contributing to the disproportionate percentage of African American males in special education?
9. Black boys often expect teachers to treat them like prima donnas, that is, the way their mothers treat them.
10. Black boys often feel that schools are out to get them and that only their mothers "have their backs," a delusion that can carry over into adult life.

The outcome of the double standard style of parenting effectively undermines the teacher's authority and effectiveness in the classroom. Parents and teachers should work as a team, not only to keep boys out of special education but to ensure that they develop into excellent, outstanding young men.

Finally, mothers consider the following:

- How long can your son stay in your house?
- What do you see in your son? Do you see a future husband, father, gainfully employed man? Whatever you see in your son, he will likely become.

In the next chapter, we will discuss the powerful impact of nutrition on students' health and school performance.

CHAPTER 10: NUTRITION

Another way to look at the acronym ADHD is not Attention Deficit Hyperactivity Disorder but A Demand for A Healthy Diet. In a recent study, the food intake of more than 3,300 children and adolescents in the United States aged 2 to 19 was analyzed. Here are the distressing high points:

- Only 1 percent of the children met all the recommendations of the food guide pyramid.
- A total of 16 percent did not meet any of the recommendations.
- Only 30 percent met the recommendations for the fruit, grain, meat, and dairy groups.
- The total amount of fat the children consumed averaged 35 percent of their total calories.
- The sugar added to foods (e.g., bread, cake, soft drinks, jam, and ice cream) averaged 15 percent of total calories.
- Nearly 50 percent of the children drank whole milk instead of low-fat milk.[57]

Education Week reports that 9 million American children are overweight. Only 25 percent of American students attend daily physical education classes. Physical activity boosts self-discipline, self-esteem, and mental alertness. A study of hundreds of thousands of California students documented that physically fit students posted higher test scores in reading and math.[58]

Throughout this book, I have tried to present as many recommendations and solutions as possible. We could reduce the number of children in special education, specifically African American males, if we did something as simple as improve their diet. Can you imagine, only 1 percent of the children studied met all the recommendations of the food guide pyramid? Sixteen percent did not meet any. This was a national study.

Consider the fact that 50 percent of African American children live below the poverty line. Visit a low-income neighborhood in the African American community and you will find that you can purchase all the liquor, pork ribs, cigarettes, and junk food you want. It is more difficult to purchase fresh, quality lettuce, broccoli, spinach, apples, oranges, and bananas.

I often watch children as they walk to school. Have you noticed what our children are eating on their way to school? Remember when your mother told you not to skip breakfast, that it was the most important meal of the day? In the United States, breakfast consumption has declined steadily over the last 25 years. Now 42 percent of children do not consume breakfast. Those who do are eating Red Hots, Pepsi, Twinkies, potato chips, and Snickers as they walk to school.

Unfortunately, children's diets do not improve much for lunch. Lunch will probably consist of hamburgers, French fries, chips, soft drinks, a baloney sandwich, and another candy bar. This menu will be repeated for dinner. Pizza or fried chicken may replace the hamburger. Again, 16 percent of children are not getting their five to seven servings of fruits and vegetables each day. It is possible for many children, particularly African American children, to go the entire day without any fruits or vegetables.

There is a relationship between nutrition and academic performance. Dr. Mary Block, in her excellent book *No More ADHD,* provides the following research:

> There was a very interesting study done in 803 New York public schools and juvenile correction facilities. In this study researchers increased fruits and vegetables and whole grains and decreased fats and sugars. Then they followed these children for a couple of years. They made no other changes

150

Nutrition

in the schools and correctional facilities during that time period, thereby assuring the accuracy of results, which were dramatic and astounding. After making these simple changes to the children's diet, the academic performance of 1.1 million children rose 16 percent and learning disabilities fell 40 percent. In the juvenile correction facilities, violent and nonviolent anti-social behavior fell 48 percent.[59]

Can you imagine that? We could reduce special education placements, increase academic achievement, and reduce disciplinary problems if we did something as simple as increase fruits, vegetables, and whole grains and decrease fat and sugar in our children's diets. Although some schools are taking out the offending vending machines that offer junk food, there are still too many schools that continue to use their vending machines to dispense fat and sugar, all in the name of profit and greed.

While our general school population is on the decline, our special education population is increasing in most schools nationwide. We could drastically change this phenomenon if we simply altered the diet by first removing vending machines, or what we sell in them, and, more importantly, providing a nutritious breakfast and lunch for students.

I am aware that some schools have attempted to provide a salad bar for lunch and that the students reject the more nutritious meals because they want to continue to consume hamburgers, French fries, and candy bars. When my youngest son was five years old, he literally refused to eat his Brussels sprouts yet thought he would still eat dessert. We politely told him that until he consumed his Brussels sprouts, there would be no dessert. He decided that he would go to bed instead. Guess what he was offered for breakfast the next day? He looked at us and smiled, realizing that we were in charge and that the next item he was going to consume would be Brussels sprouts.

We need educators who can take the role of adults and not let the children run the school. It is obvious that if children are allowed to make their own choices, the results will often not be in their best interests.

The following describes the impact of a sugar-filled diet on ADD and ADHD behaviors:

> Low blood sugar can occur in two different ways. When we eat sugar and it enters the blood stream, insulin also enters and grabs the sugar to take it to the cells to be used. This can leave too little sugar in the bloodstream, resulting in low blood sugar, or hypoglycemia. Adrenalin is then released, resulting in the symptoms most often referred to as ADHD, such as agitation, aggression, irritability, shakiness, inability to sit still, and craving of more sugar.
>
> The second way to have a low blood sugar is not to eat often enough and when you do eat, to not eat enough protein. Proteins are meats, eggs, cheese, and nuts. To protect your child from having a low blood sugar response, I have them remove all sugar, all sweets, and all white grains, such as white bread, pasta, and rice. These white grains are turned into sugar very quickly after they are eaten so the body thinks more sugar was ingested. A diet higher in protein and low in carbohydrates can help keep the blood sugar stabilize.
>
> In addition to eliminating the sugar, I recommend the child eat every three hours. This must include some form of protein with each meal or snack. Doing these two things can significantly help stabilize blood sugar levels and keep the child off the roller coaster of low blood sugar/adrenalin behaviors.[60]

Nutrition

If you would like to know more about my philosophy of nutrition, I encourage you to read my book *Satan, I'm Taking Back My Health*. Being a vegetarian for the past three decades, the last thing I would do is endorse a heavy protein diet, such as the Atkins Diet. But I do acknowledge that most of the foods that children are consuming are made of refined carbohydrates, which are filled with sugar and contribute to obesity, ADD, and ADHD. The following is another study from the George Washington University School of Medicine that makes the case:

> They gave high carbohydrate breakfasts (two slices of toasted and buttered white bread) and high protein breakfasts (two eggs scrambled in butter) to groups of hyperactive and non-hyperactive children between the ages of 8 and 13. Children in each group were given, on alternate days, a non-nutritive orange drink, sweetened. Blood samples were taken just before and up to four hours after the meals. Also, subjects took a brief test involving attention span at one-half hour, two hours, and four hours after breakfast. Results indicated that "hyperactive kids" who ate the carbohydrate breakfast and sugar drink did more poorly on the attention span test than any of the other kids in the study (they also had the highest blood sugar levels). However, when the hyperactive kids ate the protein meal, they actually did better at the attention task than even non-hyperactive groups. The upshot of this research is that parents should provide their "hyperactive and inattentive" kids with a breakfast that has a good balance of complex carbohydrates (e.g., cereal, breads, pasta), protein (e.g., milk, yogurt, cheese, eggs, lean meat, fish, poultry), and fruit, (e.g., juice, fresh fruit).[61]

When was the last time you read an IEP that included nutrition? Wouldn't it be nice if an IEP suggested a reduction in sugar and simple carbohydrates and encouraged a diet that included more complex carbohydrates and protein?

Dr. L. M. Pelsser of the Research Center for Hyperactivity and ADHD in Middleburg, the Netherlands, found that 62 percent of children diagnosed with ADHD showed significant improvement in behavior as a result of a change in diet over a period of three weeks. Simply by improving our children's diet, we can drastically reduce the placement of all children, particularly African American males, in special education.

Allergic reactions to food additives also contribute to a large number of American children in special education. Marcia Zimmerman offers the following research in her book *The ADD-Nutrition Solution:*

> The processed foods we love are loaded with over 2,800 additives that have been approved by the Food and Drug Administration. In addition, five million pounds of antibiotics in hormones are used each year to make animals grow faster and produce more milk. Common sense tells us that the overload of these items provided by the standard American diet cannot be good for us.[62]

Cow's milk, chocolate, artificial colorings, MSG, and peanuts are the leading culprits. Parents should, one by one, eliminate each of these items from their children's diet and observe their health and behaviors for one week.

First, remove cow's milk. Many African American children do not have the lactase enzyme to properly digest cow's

Nutrition

milk. One of the major causes of ear infections and mucous in so many children is the consumption of cow's milk. Almost 40 percent of children under six years old suffer chronic ear infections. Earlier we indicated the difference between boys' and girls' hearing ability. We could drastically improve boys' hearing if we simply reduced or eliminated their cow's milk consumption.

Since 1930, as mothers moved away from breast milk to cow's milk and formula, there has been an increase in the number of very young girls starting their menstrual cycle early. The hormone injections in cows are causing our children to grow at the rate of cows, not humans. The following charts are provided to further establish why we need to return to breast-feeding.

	HUMAN	COW
Casein percentage	50%	82%
Whey percentage	60%	18%
Calcium-Phosphoric	Ratio 2 to 1	1.2 to 1
Vitamin A per liter	1898	1028
Niacin per liter	1470	940
Vitamin C per liter	43	11
Reaction in the body	Alkaline	Acidic

63

COMPARISON OF THE MILKS OF DIFFERENT SPECIES

	Mean values for protein content per cent.	Time required to double birth weight (days)
HUMAN	1·2	180
MARE	2·4	60
COW	3·3	47
GOAT	4·1	19
DOG	7·1	8
CAT	9·5	7
RAT	11·8	4·5

I am not suggesting that we eliminate milk consumption. But it is often important to change the type of milk being consumed. The best is breast milk followed by soymilk, sesame seed milk, coconut milk, and goat's milk (skim, 2%, low fat).

The cost of eating nutritious foods can be high. In fact, short-term thinking sees fast food as cheaper than fruits, vegetables, and whole grains. In the long run (and even in the short term), the cost to health and pocketbook will be high. Diabetes, heart disease, and cancer have swept through the African American community like plagues. Many diseases, if not all, are preventable through diet and nutrition.

I am aware that too many African American families live below the poverty line. But it costs nothing to breast-feed. Government programs like WIC give away free baby formula, dairy, and other food products. Skip the formula and cow's milk. Breast-feed your baby. Our bodies are 80 percent water. Most children and adults are dehydrated. African American parents should reduce if not eliminate their expensive soda pop consumption and drink free water.

Artificial colorings are used in many prepared foods, such as cake mixes, butter, cheese, ice cream, crackers, soups, hot dogs, pastries, and jam. Read the labels on foods, cosmetics, and over-the-counter drugs carefully. If the label says, "natural color added," the food may be acceptable. Natural colors include annatto, carmine, and beta carotene.

Nitrates are a major water-borne pollutant. In large quantities they are neuro-toxic. Nitrates are found in chickens, hogs, and cattle in large concentrations. To reduce your consumption of nitrates and nitrites, avoid lunch meats, bacon, ham, and hot dogs, which have these chemicals added to them to retain color. Buy nitrate-free food.

Monosodium glutamate (MSG) is an additive that enhances flavor. It is often used to prepare Asian dishes. MSG readily enters the brain where it can effect the way brain cells communicate with one another. Approximately 30 percent of the people who regularly visit Asian restaurants have adverse reactions, also known as "Chinese restaurant syndrome," to MSG. As a result, many Asian restaurants now do not add MSG to their food or will withhold it upon request.

MSG presents several challenges in the African American community because we disproportionately buy more Chinese food than any other group, and many Chinese restaurants in Black communities do not provide the option of removing MSG from their food. This has major implications for our health.

Smoking is another problem in too many African American homes. Dr. Block says:

I will not see a child in my center if a parent smokes. The parent should never smoke in any of the air space the child uses, even when the child is not in the space at the time. That means never smoke in the car if the child is ever a passenger in that car, and never smoke in the house. This also means to never allow any one else to smoke in those spaces or around your child.

I cannot emphasize this enough. Smoke is a very serious toxin and the cause of many health risks for the nonsmoker as for the smoker. Smoke clings to the walls and permeates everything in the space and stays long after the cigarette, cigar, or pipe is out. Aside from the obvious health problems—lung cancer, emphysema, chronic bronchitis, and heart disease—the chemicals in tobacco smoke have been documented to cause the symptoms we think of as ADHD.

One patient did not believe that her cigarette smoke influenced her child's behavior. When I allergy-tested her child for tobacco smoke, his behavior changed dramatically. That mom never picked up another cigarette after seeing what a major negative effect it had on her child's behavior.[64]

Allergies do affect how we think, feel, and act. Conventional allergists have documented this. The medical literature is replete with the effects of allergies. Teachers, be cognizant of giving exams during the pollen season. Examining during this time discriminates unfairly against children suffering from allergies.

In *Satan, I'm Taking Back My Health,* I mention that our bodies reflect the earth. There are 103 vitamins, nutrients, and minerals in the earth, and our bodies require all of them to be properly balanced. We should strive to consume the proper

Nutrition

foods that have these 103 vitamins, nutrients, and minerals every day. Unfortunately, many Americans have a vitamin or nutrient deficiency. This is largely due to diet as well as national agricultural policies that rob the soil of life-giving nutrients.

Iron deficiency is the most common nutritional deficiency in both the United States and the world. In children, the most common cause is low dietary iron intake. Iron deficiencies can lead to behavioral problems, decreased intellectual capacity, and lower resistance to infections. I encourage parents to give children a multivitamin that contains iron.

The most common treatment for ADHD in America is drug therapy. About 80 to 85 percent of ADHD children receive drugs while only half of that number receive behavioral and educational modifications. Until this chapter, I have been arguing for behavioral and educational modifications. Now I must turn my attention to the medical profession, which chooses to prescribe drugs to children 85 percent of the time, with the drug of choice being Ritalin. The company Ciba-Geigy is the manufacturer of Ritalin. Their sales exceed $1 billion. Half of the children in special education are receiving Ritalin.

Some psychiatrists honestly admit that they seldom provide a physical exam or lab work for children before prescribing drugs, which is an atrocity. Why would any MD prescribe drugs to anyone before they actually do a test? Does Ritalin address the root problem? Do children have a Ritalin deficiency? The answer is obviously no. Children primarily have an iron, magnesium, zinc, or vitamin C deficiency, but not Ritalin. The medical profession chooses to treat symptoms rather than causes.

Under ideal circumstances, if you have high blood pressure and you take high blood pressure medicine, at some point you should no longer need the medicine. Does not the same hold true for behavioral problems and Ritalin? Count the times when you have seen a person take a medicine and after a period of time no longer need it. What we must address is the root problem, which is that only 1 percent of American children meet the necessary dietary guidelines and 16 percent do not meet any at all. Is the answer to that problem Ritalin?

Let me tell you the consequences of children who are being doped regularly with Ritalin. Dr. Mary Block associates Ritalin with kiddie cocaine. Ritalin has become the fifth leading drug consumed after nicotine, alcohol, marijuana, and cocaine. Some of the side effects of Ritalin include nervousness, decreased appetite, insomnia, stomachaches, headaches, dizziness, and drowsiness. Ritalin appears to influence mood and cause some children to cry easily and to be more socially isolated. There are even reports that Ritalin may restrict creativity.

Ritalin is a short-acting drug that is often administered in the morning. It wears off after four hours, leading to a rebound effect in the late afternoon or evening. For some kids, that consists of changes in mood, irritability, and an increase in the behavioral and attention problems that were the reason for taking the drug in the first place. In addition, Ritalin can cause skin rash, nausea, abdominal pain, weight loss, visual problems, and changes in heart rate, rhythm, and blood pressure.

Why anyone would want to take a drug with this many side effects is beyond me. There are signs near schools stressing that drugs cannot be sold or distributed within a one- to two-block radius; yet the biggest drug dealer in the community seems to be our own public school system.

The following are my recommendations for building and maintaining the health of our children:

1. Make sure that your child meets the government's minimum dietary guidelines.
2. Make sure that your child consumes a minimum of five to seven servings of fruits and vegetables every day.
3. Give your child a multivitamin.
4. Reduce all allergy-inducing foods, with cow's milk being the first suspect.

Nutrition

5. Reduce sugar and refined carbohydrates and replace them with complex carbohydrates and proteins.
6. Before children are placed in special education, they should receive a thorough medical exam—ears, eyes, blood, thyroid gland, as well as a mineral, nutrient, and vitamin deficiency test.
7. Before prescribing Ritalin, doctors should first explore all educational and behavioral modification techniques.
8. Make a physician or psychiatrist conduct a thorough medical exam before even discussing Ritalin.

In the next chapter we will look at some mainstreaming strategies that should be implemented before we dope children with kiddie cocaine.

CHAPTER 11: MAINSTREAMING STRATEGIES

As I mentioned at the outset of this book, I believe in solutions and I use the theoretical paradigm of my late mentor Dr. Barbara Sizemore—problem, causes, solutions, implementation—to help school districts around the country develop strategies for educating students. Mainstreaming strategies, as opposed to special education placement, are highly important in this process.

Throughout these chapters, I have provided strategies that were primarily focused on learning styles and gender differences. Listed below are strategies regular classroom teachers and administrators should consider before referring a child to special education.

1. Group children by gender.

✱

2. Develop shorter lesson plans.

✱

3. Assign shorter texts.

✱

4. Allow more time to complete assignments and text.

5. Allow more physical movement.

✳

6. Create learning centers.

✳

7. Develop more right-brain lesson plans.

✳

8. Implement cooperative learning opportunities in the classroom.

✳

9. Keep lesson plans simple/brief/visual/novel.

✳

10. Assign less homework.

✳

11. Assign more meaningful homework.

12. Let children stand at their desks.

*

13. Allow children to hold objects.

*

14. Play music in the background.

*

15. Pair students in a buddy system.

*

16. Identify a daily leader of the class.

*

17. Give oral exams.

*

18. Reduce the number of answers on multiple-choice exams.

19. Give open-book exams.

✳

20. Read test instructions aloud.

✳

21. Allow children to "set their stage" (greater prep time at their desks).

✳

22. Arrange preferential seating.

✳

23. Give frequent praise.

✳

24. Assist and review notebook assignments.

✳

25. Refer to students as Mr. and Miss.

26. Refer to students based on their career choices.

*

27. Start each day with, "This day in Black history."

*

28. Provide a daily word problem.

*

29. Have a positive section of the board with the students' names.

*

30. Compile positive attributes for each student.

*

31. Use rap CDs and videos.

32. Connect math to the NBA, NFL, and rap sales.

*

33. Provide chess and checkers.

*

34. Decorate the wall with student photos.

*

35. Reduce the student-teacher ratio.

*

36. Allow children to learn on the floor, sofa, and in more relaxed positions.

*

37. Encourage children to ask "why?"

*

38. Make the curriculum more culturally relevant.

Mainstreaming Strategies

39. Allow an angry student 60 to 180 seconds to calm down.

*

40. Create an area in the classroom for a student to express his anger.

*

41. Encourage students to put concepts to rap.

*

42. Provide a room of bright colors and designs.

*

43. Provide daily physical exercise.

*

44. Provide periodic exercise throughout the day.

45. Provide a martial arts class.

*

46. Always use visual aids.

*

47. Provide recess and a playground.

*

48. Allow for penmanship variances.

*

49. Allow students to print if they cannot write in cursive.

*

50. Allow information to remain on overhead projector or chalkboard indefinitely.

*

51. Provide more books on tape.

52. Allow the use of calculators.

*

53. Give brief instructions.

*

54. Avoid nagging, lecturing, arguing, sarcasm, yelling, and slipping into power struggles.

*

55. Reward good behavior.

*

56. Discuss negative behavior in private.

*

57. Ignore minor issues.

*

58. Keep your voice calm.

59. Move from a teacher-centered pedagogy to a student-centered pedagogy.

*

60. Understand that children want attention.

*

61. Allow students to water plants, care for pets, and perform other classroom management functions.

*

62. Create the maximum amount of space between each student.

*

63. Determine the best day and time for taking tests.

*

64. Avoid timed tests.

65. Position your desk in the center
of the room.

*

66. Sit with children.

*

67. Allow students a choice of assignments.

*

68. Provide assignments at different
grade levels.

*

69. Refer to tests as games.

*

70. Create a relaxed section of the room, filled
with magazines, games, audiotapes,
and videos for those who have
completed their work.

71. Enlist parent volunteers to work in class on a daily basis.

✴

72. Ignore behaviors that do not disturb others.

✴

73. Pick and choose your battles.

✴

74. Create individual and classroom rewards.

✴

75. Allow flexibility as students move from one activity to another.

✴

76. Use good eye contact.

Mainstreaming Strategies

77. Use hand signals.

*

78. Present well-prepared and organized lesson plans.

*

79. Provide time for students to get organized.

*

80. Utilize outdoors for classroom experiences.

*

81. Keep extra pencils, paper, and books in a designated area.

*

82. Assign room captains to collect homework and coordinate assignments.

83. Provide equitable response opportunities.

*

84. Provide equal feedback.

*

85. Allow Native American hand wrestling to resolve conflict.

*

86. Invite male role models on a weekly or monthly basis.

In addition, there are Africentric approaches that should definitely be incorporated into any classroom, school, and school district where there is a majority of African American students. Indeed, all students will benefit from the African approach to behavioral and educational modification.

1. Teach children the Nguzo Saba. When implemented in the classroom, these seven African values will reduce disciplinary

problems and fighting and will raise self-esteem. The Swahili words for the seven values are umoja (unity), kujichagulia (self-determination), ujima (collective work and responsibility), ujamaa (cooperative economics), kuumba (creativity), nia (purpose), and imani (faith). Put these seven principles on a poster and review on a regular basis. Some people only show the Nguzo Saba in December in celebration of Kwanzaa. These values should be taught throughout the year.

2. Maat should also be on a poster and taught throughout the year. The seven cardinal virtues of Maat are truth, justice, order, harmony, balance, reciprocity, and righteousness.

3. Unity-criticism-unity is a peer disciplinary session that uses peer pressure for positive ends. To begin, children form a circle and go around the circle praising one another. The session can also open with a chant. Next, the children who want to offer criticism raise their hands. These children then give their criticisms. The child being criticized cannot respond. We must teach children self-control. In addition, the person giving the criticism can only criticize the behavior, not the person. After all criticisms about a particular child have been heard, the child being criticized can respond. Upon completion, the students determine who was right and who was wrong. They decide, based on the range of punishments available to them, what punishment, if any, the child should receive. To close the session, children can offer praise to a particular child or each other or they can sing or chant.

These strategies, both traditional and Africentric, are important, effective ways to stem the tide of special education placements. Before another African American male child is placed into special education, the regular classroom teacher should have to implement these solutions under the supervision of an administrator. This would be included in the IEP. To avoid excessive special education placements, the wealth of information available on mainstreaming children in regular education classrooms should be studied and implemented.

CHAPTER 12: OTHER SOLUTIONS

There is no need for business as usual in public schools. Across the country, innovative and effective programs have sprung up, as a response to the evolving learning and behavioral needs of students. The following are well researched, acclaimed programs that public schools can use as a model for reducing and ultimately eliminating the flow of African American children into special education.

Pre-Referral Intervention

The first solution, the pre-referral intervention process, comes from the National Association of Black School Educators (NABSE). There is clearly a need for a step prior to special education referral, at which time instructional staff may request help with a child who exhibits an academic or behavioral problem that the teacher is unable to solve. The pre-referral intervention process is such a strategy because it prevents referrals by assisting teachers and students with the problem in the context of the general education classroom.

Although different pre-referral intervention approaches exist, they all have one important purpose: to provide supports necessary to maintain a student in general education if at all possible. The professional literature suggests that pre-referral intervention processes show promise for preventing the over-identification of African American students for special education referrals. Such processes may have potential to identify and address systemic problems (e.g., inadequate instruction, irrelevant curricula, lack of resources) and may in turn alleviate the source of students' academic and/or behavioral difficulties.

To prevent over-representation, administrators should become familiar with effective pre-referral intervention systems and institute one in their building. When functioning properly, these pre-referral intervention systems often reduce inappropriate referrals to special education and produce improved student performance. In fact, experienced practitioners report that the majority of students discussed at these pre-referral meetings are never sent to special education.

Pre-referral intervention teams go by many names, such as school-based problem solving teams, teacher assistant teams, and intervention teams. At the core of most pre-referral intervention models is collaborative problem solving among teachers, related service personnel, family members, and administrators. These individuals work as a team to provide instructional staff, with support and strategies designed to improve achievement for all students.

A major goal of a school-based referral intervention team is to improve attitudes and augment the skills of classroom teachers to adequately address students' academic and behavioral needs. The process recognizes that many variables affect learning. Thus, rather than first assuming the difficulty lies within the child, team members and the teacher consider a variety of variables that may be at the root of the problem, including the curriculum, instructional materials, instructional practices, and teacher perceptions. In general, the pre-referral intervention process is intended to:

- Document difficulties that students may be having with instruction and determine possible reasons for the problem.
- Provide and document classifications, modifications, and/or strategies.
- Assess interventions to ensure that they are appropriate and successful.
- Monitor the student's progress for a significant period of time.
- Identify students for whom learning and/or behavioral difficulties persist in spite of suggested interventions.

Other Solutions

- Differentiate the curriculum so that it is appropriate for all learners.
- Make instruction culturally relevant and appropriate.
- Adapt instruction for a wide variety of learning styles within each cultural or ethnic population.
- Staff school with experienced and culturally competent general education personnel.
- Individualize intervention strategies to reflect each student's cultural context.
- Include home-based schools and community collaborations.

Every school should develop a pre-referral team. There is good research which shows that many schools have been able to reduce the disproportionate percentage of African American children, especially boys, in special education by having a pre-referral team in place.

Early Intervention

Since well-designed early intervention programs have been shown to affect cognitive and social functioning, one would expect that those improvements would move some number of students with mild disabilities over the threshold separating those who require special supports and those who do not. Several studies measure the effect directly.

Two model demonstration programs provide data on special education placements. The Perry Preschool project reports rates of special education placement of 17 percent for program participants compared with 37 percent for control children. In the Abecedarian Project, special education placement rates differed even more dramatically for children who received the preschool program (12 percent) and the control group children (48 percent).[65]

Key School

In Indianapolis, the Key School has achieved almost celebrity status for its teacher-initiated reforms and innovations. The concept is based on Harvard psychologist Howard Gardner's theory of multiple intelligences. The Key School believes they have the most innovative education experiment in the country. Some of the ways they assess and keep records on students' development and progress include:

- Capturing each child's interests and accomplishments using videotaped portfolios. They videotape students' culminating thematic projects every nine weeks.
- Taping interviews with the students.
- Student journaling in logs about the themes of their individual projects.
- Creating nontraditional report cards that evaluate progress, participation, and motivation.

When children are involved in the educational process, when the pedagogy is student-centered and not teacher-centered, we see a tremendous reduction in special education placements.

Montessori Method

Another innovative approach is the Montessori teaching method, which uses a rich kinesthetic and experiential environment that helps children "learn to learn." Much of the philosophy centers on developing the independence of the child while creating a sense of cooperation and community.

A typical Montessori classroom is filled with interesting works, projects, and activities that relate to practical life, language, math, and social and physical development. Emphasis

Other Solutions

is placed on manipulating materials, which certainly taps into the strengths of the kinesthetic learner. Montessori classrooms are bright, appealing environments with a variety of quality materials.

The Montessori philosophy is to provide children with a variety of choices so that, within limits, children can follow a general work plan and self-directed activities. While some children work independently, others receive instruction either one-on-one or in small groups with the teacher. This approach allows a student to take a more active role in learning. For hyperactive children, greater freedom of movement in the Montessori classroom is a tremendous blessing. Public school systems can adapt and draw upon the Montessori model by implementing many of its components in their schools.

The Wimberly Initiative

In 1999, 100 Black Men of America became involved with trying to reduce the number of African American males being placed into special education. They created the Wimberly Initiative, founded by one of their late members who had served as vice president. The objective of the Wimberly Initiative was to provide Black boys with role models. The Wimberly Initiative has been implemented in several cities. The strategy includes:

- Professional development for staff, including diversity training.
- A parent-directed program to assist families to better represent their sons in IEP meetings.
- A twice-weekly after-school program to improve academic, behavioral, and social skills of students.
- Individual mentoring of Black boys.

KEEPING BLACK BOYS OUT OF SPECIAL EDUCATION

Although the program has great potential, one of their major challenges is finding consistent African American male volunteers. Schools that would like to implement the Wimberly Initiative, however, can partner with each other to maximize the time of existing volunteers and to provide an excellent service to our boys.

Charles County Public Schools
Department of Special Education
La Plata Maryland

Like other American school systems, Charles County Public Schools in southern Maryland has a disproportionately high number of African American male students in special education placements. Much of what they did in this project consisted of helping people re-frame their approach to children. They, admittedly, took a somewhat forceful approach. The "usual" process of identifying children in need of assistance is fairly straightforward; children who are failing are referred and, if there is consensus among parents and educators, testing is done to determine the need for special education services. In most cases, some deficit is to be found in a child whose failure has attracted notice, and some way is found to "assist" the child through special education placement. The special education staff is usually seen as the "ones who do that sort of thing."

They needed to re-center accountability in this process. The people who were primarily responsible for helping the unsuccessful child do better in the regular education classroom must include everybody in that school. In order to make that assertion real, the intervention team had to be available to assist both in the team's processing of the case and in the classroom. Once it was clear that they were willing to work with them, the members of the team made a similar commitment. They had to help psychologists, teachers, and administrators

Other Solutions

see that what was faced was fundamentally not a "special education problem," but rather a problem that the school as a whole needed to own and go about solving. They were much aided in this area by the good will and professionalism of everyone involved.

Teachers are trained to see failure chiefly in terms of student's disability, assessors are trained to find that disability, and special educators are trained to help the student compensate for this disability. Since the area of weakness that presents in testing, while perhaps best not thought of as disability, does, in any case, represent an area in which the student does not have particular strength, the special educator can often demonstrate something that looks like progress with remediatory intervention. Unfortunately, the remediation never quite gets the student out of the category of "special education student." Since the student probably does not suffer from any actual cognitive processing problem, the intervention will never "solve" the problem.

Following this scenario, the problem that led to the special education designation, the lace of a stimulating and embracing classroom, does not get solved, because the "special education student" designation explains the student's failure. They undertook an aggressive program to reduce this over representation in one of their middle schools. They refined their referral process and required teachers to implement and then document that they had tried differentiated instruction techniques and sophisticated behavior management with the student prior to referring him or her for special education testing. As a result, **no** students were tested or placed in special education at this school. The use of this process, paired with training and assistance, helped to reduce the disproportionate representation of African American students in special education placements by **68%**.

KEEPING BLACK BOYS OUT OF SPECIAL EDUCATION

Rites of Passage

Earlier, we discussed the showdown and power struggle that can occur between Black boys and female teachers and their mothers. The disproportionate placement of Black boys into special education also may be due to the fact that most have not matured through the rites of passage process. Most Black boys are not aware of the criteria for manhood. Unfortunately, in some neighborhoods the gang leader or Black boys themselves are defining manhood and creating their own rites of passage.

For example, many African American males have defined manhood based on how many females they have, how many babies they produce, and/or how well they can fight. In some cities, you become a man when you kill someone and go to jail. We need to redefine for boys what it means to be a man. Ironically, in "Third World" countries, boys are taught rites of passage. But in "First World" America, many boys lack rituals that symbolize progression from boyhood to manhood.

Listed below are elements that might be considered for rites of passage programs. Two books that shed light on this matter are *Coming of Age* by Paul Hill, and my book *Countering the Conspiracy to Destroy Black Boys (series)*.

1. Males should be separated from females. Boys should only be taught by men. They should be divided by age and/or grade level.
2. The logistics of the rites of passage program should be resolved, including location, day, time, and length of program.
3. Lesson plans should come from SETCLAE and the textbook *Lessons from History*.
4. Each group of boys going through the rites should have a name. We suggest Black colleges, African countries, African

groups (not tribes), or famous Black men. We discourage sports teams.

5. Manhood is based on the pyramid. The three angles represent spiritual, mental, and physical development. A good rites of passage program creates activities focusing on developing boys' spirit, mind, and body toward manhood.

6. A good rites of passage program includes activities focusing on academics, community involvement, economics, politics, history and culture, family responsibility, sex education, physical development, and values.

7. There should be opportunities to acknowledge mastery of learning.

Celebrations and rituals should culminate the rites of passage achievements.

If public schools implemented rites of passage programs, and if taught properly and consistently, we could drastically reduce the percentage of African American males in special education.

Dr. King Classroom (in-house suspension)

I recommend the Dr. King Classroom (in-house suspension). Proof of the power of his nonviolence philosophy is how schools now love Martin and celebrate his achievements on a national holiday (the third Monday in January) although many once hated him. It is important to continue to implement Dr. King's philosophies by teaching our boys to resolve conflict through nonviolence. I know it is frustrating for teachers to have so many of their male students involved in fights for nonsensical reasons: someone brushed up against them or stepped on their shoe. But we must teach African American boys, as well as all other boys, Dr. King's philosophy.

First, the school must commit to change. Establish a school policy that suspensions will be conducted at the school building. Set aside a dedicated "Dr. King" room for in-house suspensions. The room should be well lit and set up for the students to work. In-house suspension lesson plans should include the following:

1. Have students view as many movies and read as many books on Dr. King as possible.
2. Implement unity-criticism-unity.
3. View the video by Malcolm Jamal Warner, *Second Chance.*
4. View the video, *Dealing with Anger.*
5. Discuss the implications of "eye for an eye, tooth for a tooth, life for a life."
6. Read my book *Hip Hop and Maat,* especially the killing exercise.
7. View *Boys in the Hood,* and discuss the scene where the young man walks away from the skirmish.
8. Daily, make students say, "I'm sorry," "My fault," My bad."
9. Teach students the difference between a battle and a war.
10. Teach students the difference between a friend and an associate, or acquaintance.
11. Teach the Nguzo Saba and Maat.
12. Role-play someone brushing up against another person and the response of each.
13. Discuss the cultural conflict between school and street regarding behavior such as fighting, i.e., street: when someone hits you, hit them back; and school: when someone hits you, tell an authority. Discuss referees and teachers who often observe the response but not the causative action.
14. Have students read, write about, and discuss the Willie Lynch Letter (for the complete text of this infamous letter that a White slave holder wrote describing ways to make an African a slave, refer to my books *Restoring the Black Family* and *Solutions for Black America).*

Other Solutions

If the problem is not resolved in the King class, I recommend the Malcolm X class for more challenging students.

Malcolm X Classroom (in-house suspension)

1. Show videos and play audios of Malcolm X.
2. Provide books on Malcolm X for students to read, write about, and discuss. Malcolm's autobiography would be excellent for older students.
3. Provide the Willie Lynch Letter for them to read, write about, and discuss.
4. Provide cultural videos, *Scared Straight, Up Against the Wall, Boys in the Hood, Juice,* etc., to act as discussion-starters for Black male issues. Spike Lee's autobiographical movie of Malcolm would also be excellent.
5. Discuss the probability of going into professional sports, securing a rap contract, or selling drugs.
6. Teach students African American history with more emphasis on before 1620. Use *SETCLAE* and *Lessons from History.*
7. Teach students the Nguzo Saba and Maat.
8. Teach students about the stock market.
9. Teach sex education.
10. Implement martial arts.
11. Coordinate field trips to drug-abuse centers, juvenile correctional facilities, jails, prisons, courtrooms, hospital emergency rooms, and the morgue.

Fourth-Grade Intervention Team

My research has shown that from fourth grade on, Black boys' scores begin to decline. It is cheaper to correct the problem when a boy is in fourth grade than when he is in prison. Listed below are the components of a fourth-grade intervention team.

1. Identify males whose test scores have declined in fourth grade.
2. Create a support group of teachers, counselors, administrators, ministers, businessmen, and community activists who will meet with him weekly or monthly.
3. Have an encouraging meeting with the intervention team and the male student.
4. Monitor tests scores and report cards and make the necessary adjustments, whether academic, behavioral, or motivational.

Single-Gender Classrooms

Public schools should consider establishing single-gender classrooms. I encourage you to read the literature from the National Association of Single Sex Public Education (NASSPE). In the past decade, there has been government approval of single-gender classrooms. It has been accepted that they are in compliance with Title 9 legislation. As long as schools provide the same resources for females as males, single-gender classrooms are acceptable.

NASSPE has become a clearinghouse for numerous schools and hundreds of single-gender classrooms that are making fantastic gains, not only in terms of academic achievement, but also in a reduction of suspensions and special education placements. Every public school should create single-gender classrooms.

I hope that the above solutions have been helpful and that you will seriously consider implementing them in your school.

EPILOGUE

While writing this book, I met a young White female teacher who told me that she was working on her Masters in special education. I queried her to see if she fully understood the disproportionate percentage of African American males in special education. I asked, "Is one of your objectives in pursuing a Masters to reduce that percentage?"

She gave me a blank look. She said, "I don't think the placement of Black boys in special education is disproportionate. Black boys are placed for very valid reasons." I asked, "What will you learn in your graduate program that will help you mainstream boys into the regular classroom?" Another blank stare. I think she expected me and everyone else to accept the disproportionate number of Black males in special education and the futility of attempting to mainstream boys back on grade level.

I have kept that teacher in my mind's eye while writing this book, and I pray that my readers will come away with a different philosophy, ideology, and premise. In 1982, the National Research Council (NRC) report, *Placing Children in Special Education: A Strategy for Equity* made recommendations that are as efficacious and insightful today as they were then.

1. "It is the responsibility of teachers in the regular classroom to engage in multiple educational interventions and to note the effects of such interventions on a child experiencing academic failure before referring the child for special education assessment."
2. "It is the responsibility of assessment specialists to demonstrate that the measures employed validly assess the functional needs of the individual child for which there are potentially effective interventions."

3. "It is the responsibility of the placement team that labels and places a child in a special program to demonstrate that any differential label used is related to a distinctive prescription for educational practices and that these practices are likely to lead to improved outcomes not achievable in the regular classroom."
4. "It is the responsibility of the special education and evaluation staff to demonstrate systematically that high-quality, effective special instruction is being provided and that the goals of the special education program could not be achieved as effectively within the regular classrooms."[66]

There is indeed a schoolhouse to jailhouse track. There is a relationship between special education and prison, between Ritalin and cocaine, between illiteracy and incarceration. Unfortunately, mainstream White America does not see how much of their paycheck is affected by the miseducation of African American male students. It would help if White America could see on their paychecks how much is deducted for special education and prisons.

My desire is for all educators to do the right thing for African American male students. I also know that, as Frederick Douglass once said, "Power concedes nothing without a struggle." I regret that it had to take legislation and the threat of losing state and federal funds to make schools deal with this problem, and the rush toward compliance is on.

Let me close with the experience of the state of Alabama. From a negative perspective, they were forced to make changes. From a positive perspective, after being forced, they now are doing better than most states. Alabama, which has had one of the worst track records of any state in terms of statistical over-representation of African Americans in special education, agreed to extensive corrective measures. The Alabama Consent Decree included the following reforms:

A. To conduct awareness and pre-referral training. Teachers will be made aware of the tendency to refer minority students disproportionately and will receive training on how to use certain teaching and behavior management techniques that will improve learning for all students and diminish over-reliance on special education to reach children that may pose challenges in the classroom.

B. To monitor the agreement, including yearly status conferences. The state will collect data for its own evaluation and report these data to the parties.

C. To make certain changes to the Alabama Code. The IDEA encourages, but does not require, pre-referral intervention. The Alabama Code will go much further and require pre-referral intervention for six weeks in most cases before a child can be referred for special education.

D. To revamp the assessment. The new code also revises criteria for determining specific learning disabilities, emotionally conflicted as well as mentally retarded. It also requires home behavior assessments for students suspected of MR (mental retardation). Other contextual factors must be considered for all three categories to rule out other causes of low achievement that are not actually rooted in a disability.

E. To provide culturally sensitive psychometrics and training. New measures of aptitude that are culturally sensitive will be used in determining special education eligibility for minority students. Psychologists and school personnel will be trained in their proper administration.

F. To allocate funds to accomplish the decree's goal using a state improvement grant. The funds are not for changes in the decree except for the pilot of a mentoring program. Many of the changes in the decree will be funded through a state improvement grant.

G. To require reevaluation of all borderline MR students. Minority students who are borderline MR (IQ of 65 or below] or not assessed with the adaptive behavior measure) will be retested, and others will be given the option. Students who were wholly misidentified will be provided with supports and services to aid them in their transition back into the regular education classroom. Students who no longer meet the new code's criteria for MR and are deemed no longer eligible under the terms of the new agreement would be evaluated for possible placement if they were subsequently deemed eligible in another disability category.[67]

As a result of the new code, special education referrals have dropped in Alabama by 30 percent. More importantly, teachers now have a totally different understanding of how to educate the African American male child. I pray that your school, city, district, and state will not wait for a consent decree before doing justice to African American boys.

Why do Boys fight each other?

- Because they hate themselves.
- They fight people of their race because they hate their race.
- They want attention.
- The angriest boy really wants a hug and some praise.
- That is how they see their peers and family resolve conflict.
- They have low self-esteem, because they either do not know God, their history, or identified their talents and purpose in life.
- They think manhood is physical rather than mental and spiritual.
- The influence of television, video games, gangs, and rap music.
- They are frustrated because they have not experienced academic success.
- They feel fighting is their best and only strength.
- They are mad either because they are poor, absent father, and/or slum neighborhood.
- They do not know their history, they hate their present conditions, and do not feel confident about their future.
- Because of weak teachers and parents.
- They have not experienced a caring, intellectually sound, spirit-filled man.

Young children possess a quality that is essential to achieving their dreams. They know no limits. They do not know what they can't do, so they dream big dreams. They are limited only by their imagination. Research has shown that few adults can be classified as highly creative, whereas 95 percent of all four-year-olds studied were considered creative, and only four percent of all seven-year-olds studied, retain their creativity. What happened to these children? The answer is obvious. They started school and began to learn what they couldn't do.

To God be the Glory!

REFERENCES

1. Orfield, Gary. *Racial Inequity in Special Education* (Cambridge: Harvard Education Press, 2002), p. xviii.
2. Armstrong, Thomas. *The Myth of the A.D.D. Child* (New York: Penguin, 1995), p. 92.
3. ibid., p. 15.
4. ibid., p. 18.
5. ibid., p. 256.
6. op.cit., Orfield, p.6.
7. ibid., p. 25.
8. ibid., p. 45.
9. Thrasher, James. Teacher/Student Ethnicity: Suspension/ Expulsion/ Referral to Special Education. Dissertation, 1997.
10. Naglieri, Jack. "Evaluation of African American and White Children in Special Education Programs." mypsychologist.com.
11. Browne, Judith. "Derailed: The Schoolhouse to Jailhouse Track." Advancement Project, Washington, D.C.
12. Delpit, Lisa. *Other People's Children* (New York: New Press, 1995), p. 167.
13. Ladson –Billings, Gloria. *DreamKeepers* (San Francisco: Jossey Bass, 1994), pp. 21-23.
14. Porter, Michael. *Kill Them Before They Grow* (Chicago: African American Images, 1997), pp. 24-28.
15. op.cit., Armstrong, p. 235.
16. op.cit., Orfield, pp. 82, 96-97. /Donavan/Suzanne/and Cross, Christopher. *Minority Students in Special and Gifted Education* (Washington: National Academy Press, 2002), p. 171.
17. Mc Intyre, Tom, "Where the Boys Are," in Education and Treatment of Children, vol. 21, issue 3, pp. 321-332.
18. Kindlon, Dan. "Thorns Among Roses," in *Gender in Education,* pp. 163-164.

19. Freed, Jeffrey. *Right-Brained Children* (New York: Fireside, 1997), pp. 106-107.
20. Guiran, Michael. *Boys and Girls Learn Differently* (San Francisco: Jossey-Bass, 2001), pp. 113-114.
21. Foorman, Francis. "Early Interventions for Children with Reading Problems," Learning Disabilities Journal, 8, pp. 63-71.
22. Cromwell, Sharon. "Whole Language and Phonics," Education World, 1997.
23. op.cit., Freed, pp. 104-114.
24. Dunn, Rita. *Teaching Students Through Their Individual Learning Styles* (Reston: Prentice Hall, 1978), pp. 14-15.
25. op.cit., Freed, pp. 48-51.
26. Harwell, Joan. *Complete Learning Disabilities Handbook* San Francisco: Jossey-Bass, 2001), p. 17.
27. Kunjufu, Jawanza. *Black Students—Middle-Class Teachers* (Chicago: African American Images, 2002), pp. 100-101.
28. Kunjufu, Jawanza. *State of Emergency: We Must Save African American Males* (Chicago: African American Images, 2001), p. 29.
29. Dendy, Chris. *Teaching Teens with ADD and ADHD* (Bethesda: Woodbine House, 2000), p. 35.
30. op.cit., Freed, p. 55.
31. op.cit., Kunjufu, *Black Students*, pp. 97-98.
32. op.cit., Freed, p. 92.
33. Lynn, George. *Survival Strategies* (California: Underwood Books, 1996), p. 7.
34. op.cit., Dendy, p. 134.
35. op.cit., Dunn, p. 260.
36. op.cit., Armstrong, p. 111.
37. op.cit., Freed, pp. 123-124.
38. ibid., pp. 137-145.
39. ibid., p. 97.

40. op.cit., Guiran, pp. 20-26.
41. Wardle, Francis. "The Challenge of Boys in Our Early Childhood Programs," earlychildhood.com.
42. Hale, Janice. *Learning While Black* (Baltimore: Johns Hopkins University Press, 2001), p. 118.
43. Kunjufu, Jawanza. *Countering the Conspiracy to Destroy Black Boys, series* (Chicago: African American Images, 1995), pp. 18-19.
44. Murphy, Patricia. *Equity in the Classroom* (New York: Routledge, 1996), pp. 5, 178-179.
45. Ferguson, Ann. *Bad Boys* (Ann Arbor: University of Michigan Press, 2001), pp. 86-87.
46. op.cit., Kunjufu, *Countering the Conspiracy to Destroy Black Boys,* pp.91-92.
47. op.cit., *Gender in Education,* pp. 477-478.
48. ibid., p. 159.
49. ibid., p. 480.
50. op.cit., Kunjufu, *Black Students,* p. 112.
51. Epstein, Debbie. *Failing Boys* (Philadelphia: Open University Press, 1998), p. 27.
52. Bateman, Barbara. *Writing Measurable IEP Goals* (Wisconsin: Attainment, 2003), p. 4.
53. Hettleman, Kalman. "The Road to Nowhere," (Baltimore: Abell Foundation, 2004), pp. 4,16.
54. op.cit., Bateman, p. 52.
55. op.cit., Orfield, pp. 77-81.
56. op.cit., Harwell, p. 346.
57. Stevens, Laura. *12 Effective Ways to Help Your ADD/ADHD Child* (New York: Penguin, 2000), p. 45.
58. Allegrante, John. "Unfit to Learn," Education Week, December 1, 2004, p. 38.
59. Block, Mary. *No More ADHD* (Texas: Block Books, 2001), p. 84.

60. ibid., p. 70.
61. op.cit., Armstrong, pp. 68-69.
62. Zimmerman, Marcia. *The ADD Nutrition Solution* (New York: Holt, 1991), p. 71.
63. Kunjufu, Jawanza. *Satan, I'm Taking Back My Health* (Chicago: African American Images, 2001), pp. 50-51.
64. op.cit., Block, p. 102.
65. op.cit., Donovan, p. 150.
66. ibid., pp. 359-360.
67. op.cit., Orfield, pp. 175-176

INDEX

NOTES

NOTES

NOTES

NOTES

NOTES

NOTES

NOTES

NOTES